An Analysis of Brewing Techniques

An
Analysis
of
Brewing Techniques

George J. and Laurie A. Fix

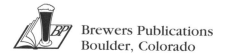

Brewers Publications
Boulder, Colorado

Brewers Publications, Division of the Association of Brewers
PO Box 1679, Boulder, CO 80306-1679
(303) 447-0816; Fax (303) 447-2825

Printed in the United States of America
10 9 8 7 6 5 4 3 2 1

ISBN 0-937381-47-0

Library of Congress Cataloging-in-Publication Data
Fix, George J., 1939–
    Analysis of brewing techniques / George Fix and Laurie Fix.
      p. cm.
    Includes bibliographical references and index.
    ISBN 0-937381-47-0 (alk. paper)
    1. Brewing—Handbooks, manuals, etc.   I. Fix, Laurie. II. Title.
TP570.F576   1997
663'.3—dc21   97-10923
                                             CIP

Technical Editor: Scott Bickham
Book Project Editor: Theresa Duggan
Copy Editor: Terri Bates Eyden
Assistant Editor: Kim Adams
Interior Designer: Vicki Hopewell
Cover Designer: Stephanie Johnson
Cover photography by Michael Lichter. Flasks courtesy of BJ's Pizza,
    Grill, and Brewery, Boulder, Colorado.
Unless otherwise noted, all interior photographs are by George and Laurie Fix.

Contents

Introduction vii

1. Wort Production..1
   Malt 1
   Cereal Grains 10
   Water 14
   Mashing Systems 22
   Hops..33
   Wort Boiling..44

2. Yeast 55
   Strains..55
   Storage 65
   Pitching Rates 68
   Propagation 70
   Oxygenation of Chilled Wort 75
   Slant Preparation and Inoculation 81
   Evaluating Pitching Yeast...84

3. Fermentation and Maturation 96
   Fermentation By-products 96
   Fermentation Vessels 104

4. Cleaning and Sanitation 109
   Cleaning Agents 109
   Sanitizers 112

5. Packaging Beer 119
   Fining Agents 119
   Filtration..126
   Carbonation 130
   Bottling Beer 137

6. Evaluation of Beer 141
    Basic Data...141
    Microbiological Analysis 144
    Evaluating Flavor 146
    Improving Competitive Judging 155

Appendix A: Basic Units 157
Appendix B: Gravity Units 160
Appendix C: pH Basics 165
Appendix D: Prediction and Measurement of RDF 171
Appendix E: Measurement of CO_2 and O_2 173
References...176
Index 181

Introduction

Welcome to *An Analysis of Brewing Techniques*. Our original intent was to write a sequel to *Principles of Brewing Science* and title it *Principles of Brewing Science II: Practical Considerations*. *Principles of Brewing Science* considered the chemical compounds relevant to beer and the reaction mechanisms associated with them. The sequel would explore the practical implications of those compounds in terms of finished beer quality. However, as our research progressed, it became increasingly clear that such material would be best organized around brewing materials and the procedures used to process them. The end result was *An Analysis of Brewing Techniques*—a practical study of brewing materials and procedures. We quote *Principles of Brewing Science* at several points in this book; however, this was done to give the reader a point of departure for a more theoretical exploration of brewing. The material referenced in *Principles of Brewing Science* is not essential to understanding the practical issues addressed in *An Analysis of Brewing Techniques*. Thus, the two books are independent of one another and can be read in either order.

The analysis of brewing materials is based on key quality indices that enable the brewer to distinguish between high-quality products and inferior ones. This information is discussed in the Malt, Cereal Grains, Water, and Hops sections of chapter 1. *An Analysis of Brewing Techniques* also compares different brewing techniques (chapter 1, Mashing Systems and Wort Boiling, and chapters 3, 4, and 5).

Chapter 2 is about yeast, and it is by far the most crucial chapter of the book. It touches on all aspects of yeast management, including available strains, yeast propagation and storage, and, most importantly, how to evaluate pitching yeast.

The five appendices deal with the measurement of key brewing variables. The procedures discussed are of great practical importance; however, they have been separated from the text in order to maintain continuity.

It is our view that brewing beer is an art—always has been and always will be. This belief defines our aspirations for beer quality. An analytical approach has value in that it helps us reach our brewing goals, such as attaining a particular flavor profile. We feel that this is as true for unorthodox brewers of idiosyncratic beers as it is for conventional beer brewers. All brewers (novice or experienced) speculate and theorize about phenomena they observe in brewing. The theme of *An Analysis of Brewing Techniques* is that progress is most uniform when such considerations are based on data.

H. Lloyd Hind, in his classic book *Brewing—Science and Practice*, notes that before there were systematic measurements, brewing was at best haphazard. He quotes Marshal Saxe (who was referring to military science in the nineteenth century): "It is a science so obscure and imperfect that custom and prejudice, confirmed by ignorance, are its foundations and support, with sacrosanct dogmas no better than maxims blindly adopted without any examination of the principles on which they were founded (Hind 1950)." *An Analysis of Brewing Techniques* was written to help brewers avoid such circumstances by taking an analytical, data-based approach to brewing. One reason brewing is so fascinating is that no one can completely master it. As our knowledge of brewing grows, so do the mysteries associated with this ancient art.

While we hope this book will contribute to the reader's insight into brewing, further reading is definitely encouraged. With this in mind, we carefully selected and used the references cited within, focusing on their accuracy, relevance, and readability.

—George and Laurie Fix

1

Wort Production

MALT

Barley Malt

Malted grains are the basis of most beers, and, indeed, beer as we know it today would not exist without the enzyme systems that form when grains are malted. A variety of grains are malted, but for most beer styles, barley is the grain of choice. The two major issues associated with malted barley are the variety and the malting process.

When we compiled research for our book on Viennese beers, we came to realize the important role that barley variety plays in beer quality (Fix and Fix 1991). It is as important to brewers as grape variety is to winemakers. The problem for brewers is that barley varieties cultivated for malting and brewing are constantly changing. For example, in 1985 Triumph, grown in northern and western Europe, and Aura, grown in West Germany, occupied the largest growing areas (*Brauwelt* 1986). Yet, by 1993, Aura and Triumph had virtually disappeared (except in France), and Alexis had become the favored spring two-row barley in England and Germany (*Brauwelt* 1993). And, undoubtedly, things will change in the future.

Barley Protein Level

Fortunately, a number of attributes are common to varieties having superior malting and brewing properties. The most important is barley protein level. De Clerck stresses this point and cites 9–11% as the preferred range (de Clerck 1957). Although introduced over four decades ago, this criterion is still widely accepted. Common beers have been successfully produced from malt in the range of 11–12%; however, malt whose protein levels exceed 12% are generally regarded as suitable only for cattle feed. Table 1.1 gives examples from the 1993 crop.

Table 1.1 Barley Protein Levels in 1993 Crop

Variety	Type	Country	Percent Protein
Alexis	Spring two-row	United Kingdom*	9.0–11.5
Alexis	Spring two-row	Germany	10.0–11.5
Triumph	Spring two-row	France	10.0–12.0
Plaisant	Spring six-row	France	11.0–12.5
Sonja	Winter two-row	Germany	12.5–13.5
Klages	Spring two-row	United States	11.5–12.5
Morex	Spring six-row	United States	13.0–13.5

*In the United Kingdom, percent protein is sometimes expressed as percent nitrogen. The conversion factor is 6.25. For example, 10% protein is equivalent to 10/6.25, which equals 1.6% nitrogen.

As table 1.1 shows, domestic malt in the United States is typically high in protein (Scheer 1990). This is traditional and closely related to the widespread use of unmalted cereal grains, such as corn and rice. High protein malt usually has enough enzymes to convert its own starch as well as the starch of the unmalted adjuncts. Since the latter does not contribute soluble nitrogen to wort, cereal grains malt in effect dilutes what would otherwise be excessive wort nitrogen levels. Nevertheless, as all-malt, craft-brewed beers and analogous seasonals grow in popularity, there will undoubtedly be an increased demand for domestic malts that have protein levels more in line with de Clerck's criterion. Thus, we are hopeful that future domestic malt will match Europe's best malts in terms of brewing quality.

The Malting Process
The malting process is also important. Indeed, a top-quality barley malted at one plant may be significantly different from the same barley malted at another plant. The entire process starts with the steep, where the barley's moisture level of a moderately modified malt is brought to 38–42% of kernel weight. For problematic barley, 46–47% is sometimes used, but this invariably produces malt with inferior brewing characteristics. Steeping takes from eighteen to thirty-six hours.

An Analysis of Brewing Techniques

The next step in the malting process is germination, which is done either on a germination floor (floor malting), as shown in figure 1.1, or in a germination compartment (pneumatic malting). It is during germination where serious modifications take place, the most important being:

- Development of the grain's enzyme systems
- Breakdown of complicated proteins into simpler structures
- Breakdown of complicated starch into simpler carbohydrates

The degree of modification depends on the type of malt being produced as well as on the brewer's requirements. However, what is important for any type of malt—well modified or otherwise—is that germination is uniform. Ideally, pulp kernels of a uniform size should result.

A number of shortcuts have been proposed to cut down on the time and cost of germinating grain, such as using higher moisture levels in the steep or adding hormones like gibberellic acid to the germinating grains. Adding hormones is banned in many countries but used in others. The danger with such stimulants is that uniformity of modification, crucial to malt quality, suffers in forced, rapid germinations.

A variety of time and temperature programs have traditionally been used in the vegetation process (i.e., steep plus germination), as table 1.2 shows. Two general trends regarding time and temperature are (1) the lower the temperature, the more uniform the modification,

Figure 1.1. Floor malting. Photo courtesy of Crisp Malting.

but it takes longer to reach the desired modification level; and (2) the higher the temperature, the required time decreases, but so will the modification uniformity.

Table 1.2 Time and Temperature Programs

Malt type	Method	Modification	Temperature	Time (days)
Pale ale	Floor	High	< 59 °F (< 15°C)	10
Pilsener	Floor	Normal	< 59 °F (< 15 °C)	8
Pale ale	Pneumatic	High	60–69 °F (16–21 °C)	4
Pilsener	Pneumatic	Normal	63 °F start–57 °F end (17 °C start–14 °C end)	7

The third and final stage of malting is drying the malt in a kiln (kilning). Malt is dried to reduce its moisture content to below 4%, since malt with higher levels tends to be highly unstable when stored. Kilning also develops color through the formation of melanoidins; the higher the temperature, the deeper the malt color (Fix, *Principles of Brewing Science* 1989). Malt enzyme systems are denatured in part during kilning, and the extent to which this occurs depends on the temperature used. Pale or Pilsener malts dried at 176–185 °F (80–85 °C) generally have strong enzyme systems capable of converting their own starch plus some adjuncts (i.e., grains without enzymes). Light amber Vienna malts dried at 185–194 °F (85–90 °C) have slightly weaker enzyme systems, as do pale ale and Munich malts dried at 221 °F (105 °C). Extreme cases are roasted malts (discussed later), whose enzyme systems have been totally deactivated.

Malting Modification Indices

A number of criteria have been proposed, and each has its strong and weak points. The following are the ones we find useful.

Assortment—A test that assesses the uniformity of kernel sizes through the use of screens. As previously noted, kernels should be uniformly plump in order to obtain highly desirable, uniform grain modification. In the United States, standard screen sizes are 7/64, 6/64, and 5/64 inches. The general rule is that at least 95% of the kernels should be captured on the first two screens. Specific examples are given in table 1.3.

Cytolysis—Cell wall modification during malting, relevant to both carbohydrate and protein modification. In particular, the viscosity of

An Analysis of Brewing Techniques

Table 1.3 Grain Assortment Data

Screen Size (inch)	European Pilsener (%)	European Pale Ale (%)	Domestic Two-Row (%)	Domestic Six-Row (%)
7/64	76.6	78.8	62.5	45.0
6/64	18.8	19.4	27.5	40.0
5/64	4.0	1.7	8.8	15.0
Through 5/64	0.6 to 0.1	1.2	0.0	0.0

standardized worts is a good indicator of the extent to which gums, such as beta-glucan, have been degraded (Banforth 1994). This tends to correlate with effective lautering and good beer filterability (Narziss 1993). Values in the range 1.4–1.5 mPas are considered desirable.

Friability, as measured by a friabilimeter, refers to the softness of the kernel (i.e., how easy it crumbles). Poorly modified malt is steely, and chewing it is akin to chewing a ball bearing. Friability above 80% is considered desirable (Wackerbauer 1986).

Proteolysis—The structural degradability of proteins. Proteolysis is subtle: too little protein modification is not desirable, but too much can negatively affect beer flavors (Narziss 1992). This is an area where mashing procedures need to be adjusted to the type of malt used (this will be discussed later). The Kolbach index—the percent of soluble protein to total malt protein that can be obtained in a European Brewery Convention (EBC) mash—is a widely used measure. In the United States, this percentage is generally expressed as the soluble to total protein ratio (S/T). While the Kolbach index and the S/T are not exactly the same, they can, for the purposes of this book, be regarded as equivalent. Table 1.4 lists some typical Kolbach values. This classic distinction of malt types has traditionally separated ale malt (Kolbach values in the low forties) from lager malt (Kolbach values

Table 1.4 Kolbach Index

Malt Type	Percent Soluble Protein
Normally modified Pilsener	34–38
Under-modified ale	37–39
Highly modified lager	> 40
Normally modified ale	42–44
Over-modified	> 45

in the mid-thirties). In recent years, the Kolbach indices of just about all malt types have been 40 or above, indicating a high degree of protein modification. The implications of this for mashing systems is explored in the section on mashing.

Another excellent measure of protein modification is a grain's free amino nitrogen (FAN) level, which also reflects a grain's amino acids—the elementary building blocks of protein molecules (Fix, *Principles of Brewing Science* 1989). Yeast fundamentally depends on malt-derived amino acids, and without them, normal beer fermentation is not possible (Ibid.). Yet, too much of a good thing is not always good. Low molecular weight proteins are foam negative, and very large FAN levels will produce this effect (Narziss 1992). They are also major players in the formation of harshly flavored fusel alcohols (Fix, *Zymurgy* 1993, 16:3). This is another area where malting and mashing need to correlate. Between the two, we need an appropriate wort FAN level, one that is not too high nor too low. Table 1.5 lists some typical malt FAN data. (This information and the Kolbach index are discussed further in Mashing Systems.)

Table 1.5 Malt FAN Levels

Conditions	FAN (mg/100 g dry malt)
Insufficient	< 120
Acceptable	135–150
Good	135–150
Very good	> 150

Extract—The total complex of carbohydrates in wort. Malt analysis sheets typically list the malt yield, the fraction of a grain's weight that is converted to extract. This is done in a standardized mash that is quite dilute (1 kilogram of malt per 6 liters of water) and is not sparged. This figure, therefore, tends to represent the maximum extract, which is neither possible nor desirable to achieve in practical brewing situations. In addition, malt yields vary—malt from two-row barley typically has higher yields than six-row barley—hence they rarely give insight into starch modification.

A more useful index of starch modification is the fine/coarse grind extract difference using a standardized mash. Low values of fine/course grind differences correlate with high levels of starch modification. Typical values are given in table 1.6.

Table 1.6 Fine/Coarse Grind Extract Differences

Percent	Starch Modification
1–1.5	High
1.5–2.0	Normal
2.0–2.2	Slightly low
> 2.2	Undermodification

Unlike protein modification, there is almost universal agreement that high levels of starch modification are desirable. As a general rule, most brewers are reluctant to use malt whose fine/course grind difference is higher than 2.2% (de Clerck 1957).

The Hartong index, sometimes used to measure starch modification (particularly on the Continent), is the extract in a 113 °F (45 °C) mash expressed as a percentage of fine-grind extract. Most brewers prefer a Hartong value of at least 38%, and values in the 38–42% range tend to correlate with good starch modification.

Kiln Temperatures—Influence the three major malt properties: the strength of its enzymes, its coloring potential, and its sulfur content. The strength of a malt's enzyme system is represented by an index called diastatic power (DP), which is usually expressed in degrees Linter (Fix, *Principles of Brewing Science* 1989). In general, diastatic power decreases as the kiln temperature increases. There is also a varietal effect: a high protein malt from six-row barley tends to have a higher diastatic power than a low protein malt from two-row barley. On the other hand, color, expressed in degrees Lovibond (°L) (or Standard Reference Method [SRM]), increases with increasing kiln temperatures. Some sample ranges are listed in table 1.7.

A malt's sulfur content is strongly affected by kiln temperature and, in general, it decreases as temperature increases. Thus, this malt

Table 1.7 Diastatic Power and Color

Malt Type	DP (°Linter)	Protein Level	Color (°L)
Domestic six-row	135–145	12.5–13.5	1.5–2.1
Domestic two–row	125–135	11.5–12.5	1.4–2.0
Pils	90–110	10.0–11.5	1.4–1.8
Vienna	50–70	10.0–11.5	3.0–4.0
Munich	40–65	10.0–11.5	5.0–7.0
Pale Ale	50–70	9.0–11.0	2.7–3.8

parameter becomes a primary issue only for pale malts. Malt has many components that contribute to the sulfur flavor in beer, but dimethyl sulfide (DMS) is the component that is generally monitored. This compound is created in wort production from malt precursors, and it is the DMS precursor level of malt that is most relevant (Fix, *Principles of Brewing Science*, 1989; Fix 1992, 15:3). Table 1.8 gives typical values.

Table 1.8 Malt Sulfur Levels

Malt type	Level (micrograms per gram of malt)
Pale ale	1–2
Modern Pilsener	5–6
Domestic two-row	6–8
Domestic six-row	8–10

It is important to emphasize that sulfur flavor in beer is very subtle. Selective gram-negative bacteria can create large amounts of DMS, leaving an unpleasant cornlike/cooked vegetable taste in beer. Domestic six-row malt also leaves a cornlike flavor, unless special steps are taken in wort production to reduce DMS levels. In striking contrast, select German pale lagers often have a highly pleasant malty/sulfury flavor profile. A variety of sulfur components contribute to this, DMS being just one.

Wheat Malt

Wheat malt is completely different from barley malt. First, protein levels in wheat malt are typically high. It is not unusual to find values in excess of 13% (Oloff and Piendl 1978). Certain varieties grown in special microclimates result in wheat malt protein levels in de Clerck's range of 9–11%, but these are the exception and not the rule (de Clerck 1957). In general, soft white wheat varieties have lower protein levels than hard red wheats. Values for fine-grind (laboratory) extract are usually higher than those of barley malt. For the most part, this is a consequence of wheat malt not having husks. As a result, carbohydrates occupy a higher fraction of grain weight. This extra yield is rarely seen in practical brewing situations, and many brewers find they get lower yields from malted wheat than from malted barley. One reason for this is that problems are encountered in malting wheat. Typically, cytolytic modification is low, hence viscosity is high.

Values in the range of 1.8–1.9 mPas are not uncommon (as compared with 1.4–1.6 for malted barley) (Oloff and Piendl 1978). In contrast, proteolytic modification is high, and resulting Kolbach values are generally over 40%. In order to avoid the vicissitude of excess protein modification, wheat malt is usually processed in such a way that carbohydrates are undermodified. Differences in fine/coarse grind extract are often above 2.5%, which tends to relate to low yields in practical mashing systems.

Roasted Malt

Roasted malts play an important role in brewing, both for their coloring potential and for their special flavoring. In the roasting process, the enzyme systems of these malts are totally deactivated. As a consequence, they are often called adjunct malts. The market is saturated with trade names, thus the simplest way to classify roasted malts is by the two ways in which they are produced:

- Group 1: Green malt (germinated but not dried)
- Group 2: Regular malt (germinated and dried)

The flavoring of these malts differs from pale malts, primarily because of the Maillard products formed during roasting. Maillard products are N-heterocyclic compounds, such as pyrazine and pyrazole (Fix, *Principles of Brewing Science* 1989). According to Narziss, these compounds can vary in magnitude depending on the length of time the malt is roasted and on the roasting temperature (Narziss, *Zymurgy* 1993). Lightly roasted malts have a sweet toffee/caramel taste; highly roasted malts have a burnt taste often accompanied by sharp/acid tones. Tables 1.9 and 1.10 provide data from Blenkinsop's research (Blenkinsop 1991).

Table 1.9 Group 1: Green Malt

Malt Type	Color (°L)	Taste
U.S. light (CaraPils)	5–8	Toffee/caramel
European light	13–17	Toffee/caramel
Crystal	30–40	Caramel/nutty
Crystal	70–80	Nutty/roasted
Dark crystal	100–160	Toffee/burnt

Table 1.10 Group 2: Regular Malt

Malt Type	Color (°L)	Taste
Amber	50–60	Bitter/burnt
Chocolate	450–500	Slightly sharp/acid dry
Black	500–550	Slightly sharp/acid dry

Brown malt, used in traditional porter formulations, falls into the group 2 amber category (Bergen 1993). It is roasted with direct heat from beech, oak, or other wood fires. Malt used for Bamberg-style rauchbier is produced similarly. Maillard products formed during this roasting process are highly complex and not yet completely defined, and the flavors they impart are equally complex.

Brewers often overlook the limited shelf life of roasted malt. Their unique aromatic compounds, which can be used to great advantage with fresh malt, are the first to suffer in extended malt storage. This is particularly true of crystal malt, or caramel malt. Unpleasant, cloyingly sweet caramel flavor tones are signs of deterioration. Diacetyl, even at low levels, will tend to amplify these negative flavor notes, as will oxidation.

CEREAL GRAINS

There are two basic reasons to use unmalted grains. First, cereal grains (corn, rice, etc.) tend to have the same carbohydrate structure as malt but are often cheaper; therefore, selected use of these grains can save the brewer money. The second and more interesting reason to use them is that while cereal grains do have a definite protein content, they tend to make only minimal contributions to the wort's protein pool. Thus, cereal grains used in conjunction with malt give extra strength to the finished beer without the satiating effects that result when only malt is used to gain extra gravity. Some world-class lagers and ales are produced this way (Fix 1994; Protz, *Real Ale* 1991).

Gelatinization and Saccharification

The classic concern about unmalted grains is the fear of incomplete gelatinization and saccharification. Narziss correctly points out that if these defects are present, the finished beer can have "broad bitterness" and a "raw character" (Narziss, *Brauwelt* 1993, 3). Flaked grains are gelatinized by passing the grains through hot rollers at 185 °F (85 °C). This is nearly ideal for grain gelatinization, and the concerns expressed by Narziss generally do not apply to these grains. In particular, they are readily converted in normal mashes at usual saccharification temperatures (i.e., 140 °F [60 °C] or above). Yields in excess of 80% can be expected with these grains.

Raw grits require a cooker mash in order to achieve gelatinization. Boiling times vary from fifteen minutes for refined corn starch and refined grits up to forty-five minutes for common grits. A 10% malt charge is typically used, and cooker mash thickness is usually maintained with feed water during boiling to compensate for evaporation and water uptake by the grains.

Narziss also stresses the importance of proper mashing procedures to avoid incomplete gelatinization and saccharification (Narziss, *Brauwelt* 1993, 3). The best results are obtained when the mash pH ranges from 5.5–5.6. Lower values typically lead to high wort viscosity.

Storage

The oil content of cereal grains is a concern, more so for corn products than for rice. Oil can become rancid during extended and/or high-temperature storage. Today, products are usually produced in such a way that the oil content is below 1%. Brewers should request this information from suppliers to avoid storage problems. It should also be noted that high oil levels in cereal grains generally lead to inferior beer foam.

Cereal Grain Types

A number of unmalted cereals are used in brewing, the most common being flaked maize, refined corn grits and corn starch, corn grits, rice grits, unmalted barley, wheat adjuncts, and rye adjuncts.

Flaked Maize—Although it is one of the most expensive grains, flaked maize is by far our favorite unmalted grain. This grain is pregelatinized and can be added directly to the mash. Since the flakes do not contribute to the wort's protein pool, they are normally added once saccharification temperatures are reached. Flaked maize was once widely used by brewers in the United States, but its high cost has led to diminished use (Fix 1994; Nugy 1948). Flaked maize, however, is still very popular with brewers in Belgium and the United Kingdom where it is valued for the soft and subtle grainlike sweetness it imparts. We have obtained yields close to 80% from flaked maize.

Wort Production

Refined Corn Grits and Corn Starch—These products are pre-processed by wet-milling procedures and are essentially pure starch. As a consequence, yields from these products are often above 90%. They require cooking in order to achieve proper gelatinization, however boil times are brief, typically five to fifteen minutes. Dextrose is produced from refined corn grits and corn starch by further processing, where the starch is degraded into glucose. When refined grits are mashed, they have a carbohydrate spectrum similar to that obtained from malt.

Corn Grits—Corn grits are the cheapest and most widely used adjunct in the United States. They are a by-product of the food industry and are produced by a dry-milling process. Typically, thirty to forty-five minutes of boil time are required in a cooker mash, and yields are similar to those of flaked maize.

Rice Grits—This rather expensive grain has long been esteemed by U.S. brewers as the perfect adjunct. Rice grits tend to impart a clean, neutral flavor that does not interfere with malt flavor. These grains are produced the same way as table rice, that is, by separating the starchy endosperm from the outer layers (husk, bran layers, and germ). The kernels are often broken in the milling process and are not used as table rice because of physical appearance. These "rejects" are normally sold as brewers' grits. Short-grain rice is preferred because medium- and long-grain varieties can lead to viscosity problems in cooker mashes. Even the short-grain products are milled in the brewery to get a uniform, small granule size. For these, a fifteen-minute boil is sufficient to achieve gelatinization; longer boiling can lead to viscosity problems. Yields are similar to those of flaked maize and corn grits. Rice is also available in flakes, but rice flakes have not been as widely used as flaked maize.

Unmalted Barley—This adjunct has long been of interest to brewers because of its similarity to malted barley. For example, unlike rice or corn, unmalted barley definitely contributes to the wort's protein pool. It has been estimated that approximately 15% of unmalted barley protein is dissolved in the wort (Fix 1985). This is lower than the amount of protein obtained from malted barley (around 35–45%), but much higher than the minimal amounts contributed by corn or rice adjuncts. Experience shows that if unmalted barley is mashed with a suitably high concentration of malt, the proteins will be foam positive.

Pregelatinized flakes are the easiest form to use. While they are ready for saccharification, there is, nevertheless, the problem of barley gums, like beta-glucan, that must be dealt with in mashing (Fix, *Principles of Brewing Science* 1989). The appropriate breakdown of beta-glucans can be achieved with a low-temperature rest in the mash (preferably around 104 °F [40 °C]) where beta-glucase activity is encouraged. The use of low protein, plump unmalted barley is also recommended to avoid the excessive wort viscosities that result from barley gums.

Unmalted barley is sometimes roasted, so it has traditionally been an important component of many stout formulations. It is very similar to highly roasted black malt, except that its flavoring tends to be more intensely sharp/burnt/acidic.

Wheat Adjuncts—It is a well-known fact that foam-building properties of wheat proteins are superior to those of barley. This effect has been exploited by brewers who use a small wheat charge to the grain bill to increase the foam quality of beer—a practice that is something of an art. At too low a level, the increase in foam quality is generally too trivial to justify the effort. On the other hand, wheat proteins typically do not respond well to chill-proofing agents, so too high a level can result in a reduction of the beer's resistance to chill haze. Decades ago, malted wheat was widely used as a foam-building agent. However, given the high degree of proteolytic modification of modern wheat malt, unmalted wheat is now preferred.

In addition, unmalted wheat adds a discernible smoothness to finished beer. A striking example is Belgian-style white beer, where up to 50% of the grain bill consists of unmalted wheat (Lodahl 1994). There are also several English-style amber ale formulations that use wheat, some with charges as high as 20%. With a wheat charge of 50%, it is important to use barley malts with diastatic powers above 120 °Linter; with a 20% wheat charge, diastatic powers of 90 °Linter are needed.

Rye Adjuncts—Rye imparts a distinctively crisp and slightly spicy character to beer. Interest in the grain has been growing, which has led to a new beer style—American rye ale. This ale differs from roggenbier (German-style rye beer) in much the same way that American wheat ale differs from German weisse beer. American rye ale is typically made with a 10–20% charge of flaked unmalted rye, and it tends to have a dry, snappy finish. We find it a good deal more interesting than the average American wheat ale.

Flaked rye has many of the properties of flaked barley. It definitely contributes foam-positive proteins to wort. Also, its beta-glucan content is high, hence a temperature rest near 104 °F (40 °C), or at least one well below 140 °F (60 °C), is recommended.

Rye is also available as a malted grain, however, constituents derived from rye husks have a strong, spicy and bitter taste, so use caution. Another advantage of flaked rye is that it is dehusked.

WATER

There has always been something of a mystique surrounding beer and the water used to brew it. It has often been claimed that the historically successful brewing centers gained their fame because of their water. Even today, select brewers assert in their advertisements that "it's the water" that is responsible for the special qualities of their beers. But the fact is, most of the world's best beers are brewed with water that has been extensively treated. While today's water-treatment programs lack the romance attributed to older brewing procedures, they do, without a doubt, offer a shorter path to consistent beer quality. We will review some of the major procedures used to produce brewing liquor (i.e., treated water that has been rendered suitable for brewing).

The first issue to address is water purity. Contaminates fall into four categories: (1) inorganic material, (2) organic material, (3) microbes, and (4) miscellaneous particulates. Heavy metals are the greatest concern. Table 1.11 lists the maximum acceptable levels; water not meeting these requirements is unsuited for brewing.

Table 1.11 Maximum Acceptable Metal Levels in Brewing Water

Element	Concentration (mg/L)
Copper (Cu)	0.100
Iron (Fe)	0.050
Lead (Pb)	0.050
Manganese (Mn)	0.100
Mercury (Hg)	0.002
Zinc (Zn)	0.500

While levels higher than the concentrations listed in table 1.11 will have a negative impact on yeast and adversely affect beer stability, sublimated levels can have positive effects. Zinc is the best understood example. Zinc concentration in wort is derived primarily from malt and possibly from the brewing liquor. At a level of 0.1–0.2 milligrams per liter, zinc plays a vital role in fermentation. In particular, it is a crucial cofactor for carbon splitting, which is enzymatically induced by yeast during respiration (Fix, *Principles of Brewing Science* 1989). When barley crops are known to be poor, low zinc levels in wort are not uncommon, which can lead to a number of disorders (Piesley 1977). Brewers who use a high fraction of unmalted cereals in standard gravity batches typically experience zinc deficiencies. Zinc sulfate ($ZnSO_4$) is often added to correct this.

The copper content of wort is a more subtle issue. It has been clearly shown that copper is toxic to yeast above 10 milligrams per liter. Also, at or above 1 milligram per liter, copper serves as a catalyst of oxidation, leading to permanent haze (Moll 1979). In contrast is the anecdotal evidence of brewers who experience elevated beer sulfur levels in breweries where there is no wort contact with copper (Miller 1993).

Organic residuals are feared because of their foul flavoring and also because they provide food for microbes. Most water supplies are chlorinated to prevent or at least control these effects. Nevertheless, from a brewing perspective, many water supplies cannot be viewed as sanitary. To make matters worse, residual chlorine will react with organic material to create products that are very harmful to beer flavor.

A number of measures have been used to control water contaminants, but in the final analysis, some form of water filtration is the most effective means. Here are the best options:

(1) Activated carbon filtration works by absorption, and it is usually used with silver impregnations to provide antimicrobial effects. This is the best filtration system to remove chlorine, organics, and residual particulates, like sand and dust.
(2) Reverse osmosis is a series of membrane filtrations that effectively removes organics, inorganics, and microbes. It also removes some water minerals, although generally it leaves water chlorine levels unchanged.
(3) Deionization is a two-stage process whereby water minerals are exchanged with hydroxide and hydrogen ions. This process also removes organic and inorganic residuals as well as microbes. As with reverse osmosis, water chlorine levels are generally unchanged. It should also be noted that many home water softeners use only the first part of the deionization process, where

calcium ions are replaced with sodium ions. Such systems are not suitable for processing brewing liquor.

The most widely used water filtration system in brewing consists of (2) or (3), followed by option (1) to remove chlorine. Such water is ready for general use, for cleaning, and for rinsing equipment. Since it has no residual protection against microbial infection, great care should be taken on a regular basis to ensure brewery water lines are sanitary.

Water that has been filtered still may not be suitable for brewing. The final step is to adjust the mineral content of the water in ways that are favorable to the type of beer being brewed. The most relevant cations (positively charged ions) are calcium, magnesium, and sodium. Salts are combinations of these with anions (negatively charged ions). The most relevant are bicarbonate, sulfate, and chloride.

Water hardness has traditionally referred to the ability of soap to form suds; the harder the water, the less suds. Hardness is correlated to the calcium and magnesium content in water. Today, hardness is reported as the sum of these ions measured as an equivalent amount of calcium carbonate. It can be computed with the following:

$$\text{hardness } CaCO_3 = 5/2 \times <Ca^{++}> + 25/6 \times <Mg^{++}>$$

where $<Ca^{++}>$ and $<Mg^{++}>$ are the calcium and magnesium concentrations in ppm (milligrams per liter). Calcium carbonate has a molecular weight of 100, while that of calcium is 40. Their ratio, which is *100/40 = 5/2*, is the first coefficient in the formula. The coefficient *25/6* is the ratio of the molecular weight of calcium carbonate to that of magnesium. These coefficients convert the ion levels into an equivalent amount of calcium carbonate.

Alkalinity refers to the number of alkaline ions present (most notably bicarbonates) in the water. It is typically determined by titration.

Pure water supplies can differ dramatically with respect to mineral content, hardness, and alkalinity, as illustrated in table 1.12. Sample 1 is spring water from Ann Arbor, Michigan, and is characterized by a high carbonate hardness (i.e., high levels of calcium, magnesium, and bicarbonate). Sample 2 is artesian water from Pittsburgh, Pennsylvania. It is also hard, but unlike sample 1, it has much lower bicarbonate levels. Water like sample 1 is sometimes called "temporarily hard water," because if it is boiled for a sufficient length of time, the calcium ions will complex with the alkaline material and precipitate out as calcium carbonate. This, of course, will reduce both the hardness and alkalinity of the water. Since the bicarbonate content of sample 2 is much lower than sample 1, boiling will lead to a lower reduction of hardness. As a consequence, water like sample 2 is often called "permanently hard water."

Table 1.12 Mineral Content of Pure Water Samples

Element	Sample 1*	Sample 2	Sample 3
Calcium (mg/L)	141.8	88.0	9.6
Magnesium (mg/L)	38.1	48.0	2.4
Sulfate (mg/L)	97.6	199.0	29.0
Chloride (mg/L)	90.0	348.0	14.0
Bicarbonate (mg/L)	409.0	46.0	25.0
Alkalinity (as $CaCO_3$)	335.0	74.0	16.0
Hardness (as $CaCO_3$)	514.0	417.0	34.0
pH	7.1	6.9	7.5

*Sample 1 is spring water from Ann Arbor, Michigan; Sample 2 is artesian water from Pittsburgh, Pennsylvania; and sample 3 is public water from Arlington, Texas.

Water samples 1 and 2 were remarkably free of pollution, and the problematic contaminants cited previously were absent. Neither of these samples was filtered, and the data given in table 1.12 represent the samples as collected at the source. Unfortunately, this is not always the case for artesian and spring water, and brewers using water from such sources should have it carefully analyzed for purity.

Sample 3 is from civic water supplies in Arlington, Texas. Samples from the tap typically have residual microbes (more during warmer months), organic matter, and chlorine. While sample 3 meets Environmental Protection Agency drinking water standards, it is unsuitable for brewing. The data shown in table 1.12 represent water after filtration ((1) and (2) discussed previously). This treatment almost completely removed minerals, and water like sample 3 is regarded as soft.

The water samples in table 1.12 roughly parallel the differences seen in water (untreated) from classic brewing centers. Selected examples are given in table 1.13. Munich water, like sample 1, is temporarily hard. Water like this can also be found in Dublin and London.

Wort Production

The samples from Dortmund and Pittsburgh (sample 2) are considered permanently hard, while Pilsen water and the treated water (sample 3) are soft.

The big question is how mineral content affects the brewing process. While stylistic considerations come into play, the most important are the effects water has on mash and wort pH. For the many reasons we will discuss in the next three sections, for most beer styles it is highly desirable to achieve a mash pH of 5.2–5.4 and a wort pH of 5.0–5.3. Following are the relevant mechanisms:

(1) Interactions between calcium and malt phosphates increase the mash hydrogen ion content and, hence, lower the pH. This mechanism is also present in wort boiling.
(2) Bicarbonates act as a buffer to any change in mash pH.
(3) Acids present in malt tend to lower pH, which increases as malt color increases. One can also directly acidify the mash (or mash water) to achieve the same effect.

Given a particular water supply and a grain bill, these mechanisms compete to determine the mash pH and, later, the wort pH. Therefore, the question is what steps can be taken to ensure pH falls into the desired range. We have found that Kolbach's criteria have proven to be the most useful in this area (Kolbach 1953). In particular, he introduced a notion of residual alkalinity (RA), defined as:

$$RA = <HCO_3^+> - <Ca^{++}>/135 - <Mg^{++}>/7.$$

He then showed that the mash pH will increase or decrease as the residual alkalinity is increased or decreased. The approximate rule is that a change in residual alkalinity of 180 milligrams per liter as calcium carbonate (hardness) equals a change in pH of 0.3.

To see how these concepts can be used, consider sample 3 in table 1.12. For pale beers, mash and wort pH fall into the desirable range if $<Ca^{++}>$ equals 50 to 150 milligrams per liter and residual alkalinity is less than 50 milligrams per liter as calcium carbonate. In sample 3,

$$RA = 25 - (9.6)/35 - (2.4)/7 = 24.4 \text{ mg/L as } CaCO_3.$$

This comfortably satisfies the criterion that residual alkalinity be less than 50 milligrams per liter as calcium carbonate. The calcium content

Table 1.13 Classic Brewing Center Water Supplies

Element	Munich	Dortmund	Pilsen
Calcium (mg/L)	75	225	7
Magnesium (mg/L)	18	40	2
Sulfate (mg/L)	10	120	5
Chloride (mg/L)	2	160	5
Bicarbonate (mg/L)	150	180	15
Hardness (as CaCO$_3$)	262	730	26

typical of soft water does not meet the specified criterion. The most common procedure is to add calcium chloride hydrate salts. Calculations show that the addition of 20 grams per hectoliter (0.8 ounces per barrel) will increase the calcium level by 50 milligrams per liter (Fix, *Principles of Brewing Science* 1989). Gypsum is sometimes used, and here, 22 grams per hectoliter (0.88 ounces per barrel) have the same effect.

The above consideration requires modification when the fraction of dark malts in the grain bill increases, since these malts bring extra acidity to the mash. In this context, calcium carbonate hydrate salts are often used, and the addition of these at 25 grams per hectoliter (1 ounce per barrel) will increase the calcium level by 50 milligrams per liter. Clearly, stylistic considerations (discussed later) come into play, but as a general rule, with worts color in the range of 10–15 °L, a mixture of calcium chloride (or gypsum) and calcium carbonate should be used. For darker worts, the exclusive use of calcium carbonate is recommended.

Water sample 1 in table 1.12 brings up entirely different issues. Here, the residual alkalinity is quite high; in fact,

RA = 409 - 141.8 / 35 - 38.1 / 7 = 399.5 mg/L as CaCO$_3$.

Kolbach's rule would suggest that for pale beers the pH will be too high, by around 0.6. In test brews, using this water with pale malts led to mash pH levels in the range of 5.75–5.9, which is unacceptable. Since the calcium context of this water is fine, it is usually best to consider reducing the bicarbonate level for pale beers. One way to do this is through deionization, which will create the same situation as in water sample 3 in table 1.12.

Acidification water (or mash) is an alternative. In Bavaria, where water like sample 1 is common, the old practice of biological acidification of the mash has reemerged as a serious and widely used procedure (Oliver and Daumen 1988, 3). However, it is a tricky procedure, and only special strains of bacteria can be used (Oliver and Daumen 1988, 4). It is crucial that these microbes create only lactic acid and no other products. While the microbes used will typically be killed in the boil, their products, on the other hand, tend to spill over to the finished beer.

The addition of food-grade acids to the brewing liquor is more common. This procedure has to be approached empirically, since water pH and mash pH do not always correlate. In water like sample 1, we have found that 0.1 liter per hectoliter (1 gallon per 1,000 gallons) of 50% lactic acid suffices. This is reduced to 0.06 liter per hectoliter (1 gallon per 1,600 gallons) if 85% phosphoric acid is used. The exact amount needed depends on the residual alkalinity as well as on other factors.

As the color of the wort increases, water like sample 1 becomes more attractive in its native untreated state. It was reported that a turn-of-the-century brewery in Ann Arbor made sensational dark ales and lagers with this spring water (*Ann Arbor News* 1975), and this has been our experience with test brews as well.

Water sample 2 in table 1.12 also requires different considerations. Like sample 1, this water is hard, but with a much lower residual alkalinity:

$$RA = 75 - 88 / 35 - 48 / 7 = 65.6 \text{ mg/L.}$$

Water like this can be used untreated for a variety of pale ales, light amber ales, and lagers. However, test brews indicate less than inspiring results when the wort color goes much above 6–8 °L. In this case, deionization is the only viable option, followed by the measures described previously for dark worts and soft water.

The most common stylistic issue concerns the use of calcium chloride versus calcium sulfate (gypsum). The chloride ions generally promote beer smoothness, while sulfates tend to promote a harsh hop bitter and drying aftertaste in beer. Thus, calcium chloride tends to be used widely in modern brewing, particularly with more delicate beer styles. There is, however, one major and important exception— Burton ales. The composition of Burton's water is given in table 1.14, and, as can be seen, the sulfate level is much higher than in the previous examples. The effect on finished beer flavors is striking. In England, this is often called the "Burton sulfur taste" (Protz 1991), but it is significantly different from sulfur flavors derived from organic sulfur constituents like DMS. It has a decidedly mineral tone, but it interacts with the high level of Goldings hops that are used in a very unique way. Water like this would be a disaster for most ale and lager formulations, but it is largely responsible for Burton's fame as a brewing center.

Table 1.14 Burton Water

Element	Level (mg/L)
Calcium	275
Magnesium	40
Sulfate	450
Bicarbonate	260
Chloride	35

A stylistic issue with Pilsener formulations is whether or not to treat soft brewing water with salt. The archtypal Pilsener, Pilsner Urquell from Pilsen, uses the soft water shown in table 1.13 as is. In the United States, selected small regionals (e.g., the Straub Brewing Co., St. Marys, Pennsylvania [Fix 1982]) have done the same. There is a loss of efficiency in wort production (most notably in yields), but the flavoring of the finished beer is indeed quite special. In particular, we found in test brews with various Pilsener formulations that water like sample 3 produces a softer finish if untreated.

In Germany both hard water and soft water Pilseners are brewed. König Pils from Duisberg is a widely praised example of a hard water Pils. The water at Duisberg is very similar to that of nearby Dortmund. On the other hand, Veltins, another Rhinelander Pilsener, is a marvelous example of a soft water version. The direct comparison of these world-class beers is an excellent way to get a measure of the effects of brewing water.

The effect of bicarbonate is somewhat contradictory. This mineral tends to promote a rounded malt flavor, but at the same time, a sharper and harsher hop bitterness. Traditionally, the moderately hopped sweet stouts of London and the Munich-style darks exploited these effects to great advantage.

Still unresolved is the role sodium ions play. Many experts assert that sodium ions have no effect, while others assert that they promote smoothness, particularly if the water comes from a sodium chloride environment. Our experience has been completely to the contrary, particularly if sodium levels are 75 milligrams per liter or higher. We found a broad harshness not found in equivalent brews made with water having lower sodium levels. Moll reports similar results (Moll 1979).

MASHING SYSTEMS

From a conceptual point of view, mashing is best seen as an extension of malting in that it continues the carbohydrate and protein modification (degradation) started in malting. The main differences are the times and temperatures involved. Because of this, choosing the best mashing system depends a great deal on the way the grains have been malted.

Choosing the Best Mashing System

There are a number of parameters that can be used to measure the effectiveness of mashing systems. The most important are carbohydrate yield, percent fermentability, maltose/maltotriose ratios, and protein levels.

Carbohydrate Yield—In addition to modifying grain carbohydrates, we also need to dissolve them in the mash. This is a three-stage process whereby starch molecules (1) take up water (liquefy), (2) rupture (gelatinize), and (3) disperse into the medium. The efficiency of the mashing system determines the yield obtained. Yield is the percent of the grain's weight that goes into extract dissolved in the mash (this and related units are discussed in appendix B). Generally, yields in the 60–70% range can be expected (problems that lead to deviations are discussed later).

Percent Fermentability—Not all of the extract dissolved in the mash can be metabolized by yeast. Moreover, the type of mashing system used strongly influences how much fermentable extract is actually obtained. The relevant parameter is the real degree of fermentation (RDF). (RDF is discussed in appendix D, as is a forced fermentation procedure for measuring it.) Most mashing systems produce RDFs in the range of 63–67%. However, many Bavarian lagers as well as some strong ales have values below 60%. Low-calorie beers, on the other hand, usually have RDFs in excess of 70%. Thus, the optimal value of RDF depends on stylistic issues.

Maltose/Maltotriose Ratios—Theoretically, maltose and maltotriose are both fermentable sugars. Most lager strains take in both sugars with equal ease, and the ratio of these sugars is not very important. Selected ale strains, on the other hand, behave quite differently. The uptake of maltotriose is much slower than that of maltose, and the metabolism of the former may be incomplete. Test brews show that for such strains, the ratio should be above 3:0. In cases where the ratio dropped below 3:0, the RDF actually achieved was lower than predicted by the procedure in appendix C, which means there were fermentable sugars left in the finished beer. This is not desirable, because the beer's balance will be skewed, and because residual sugars could support undesirable microbial activity.

Proteins Levels—As with carbohydrates, we want to dissolve malt proteins as well as appropriately modify them. In this context, a definite balancing act is required. There are three groups of proteins. The most complicated are the high molecular weight proteins found in unmalted barley and wheat. Their major function in beer is to interact with malt phenols and to create haze; therefore, it is advantageous to degrade these proteins or to remove them by mechanical precipitation. The next level down in complexity are the medium molecular weight proteins. These are highly favorable in that they play a constructive role in beer foam (see chapter 5's discussion of carbonation), and they also play an important (but poorly understood) role in the quality of the beer's malt flavor. The last group consists of amino acids, the building blocks of all proteins, (Fix, *Principles of Brewing Science* 1989). Amino acids have both positive and negative effects. They are a crucial source of nitrogen for yeast, and deficiencies in the finished wort can lead to disordered fermentations (Ibid.). On the other hand, unmetabolized amino acids that spill over into beer are foam negative. In addition, some yeasts (particularly nonculture strains) tend to use the carbon skeletons of excess amino acids to metabolize harshly flavored fusel alcohols (see chapter 3). As already mentioned, FAN is the unit used to measure amino acid content. Experience has shown that FAN levels in wort need to be above 150 milligrams per liter and preferably over 250 milligrams per liter, for a sufficient amount of amino nitrogen to be available for yeast metabolism. However, values in excess of 350 milligrams per liter can cause problems. Fortunately, FAN levels can be strongly influenced by mashing programs, so this is an area where brewers have some control.

Mash pH

One of the most important operational variables in the brewer's control is the mash pH. As noted in the previous discussion about water, the mash pH, for all practical purposes, is determined by the water mineral content and the grain bill. Our experience, with a large number of test brews, is that pH is established very early in the mash and is buffered from that point forward. Moreover, we found it important to have a pH below 5.5 for all malt worts. Theoretical considerations using mathematical models indicate that this condition is necessary for proper enzymatic activity. This was confirmed in test brews having a high pH in the mash, with values in the range of 5.6–5.9 leading to erratic results. The yields varied considerably (usually on the low side), and control over RDFs was weak. The fact that a high mash pH may lead to a high wort pH is also a problem (this will be discussed shortly).

Temperature Programs

Assuming that a proper pH has been established, a brewer's primary control comes with the time and temperature program used. Following are some general guidelines for various temperature ranges and their effects.

(1) A rest in the range of 95–104 °F (35–40 °C) has traditionally been called an acid rest. We find this term to be somewhat misleading, because the pH in test brews was not greatly affected, at least for rests of thirty minutes or less. Nevertheless, a number of desirable activities do occur in this temperature range. For example, it is optimal for beta-glucanase, which leads to a better modification of gums, such as beta-glucans, which in turn improve lautering as well as beer filterability. The major amylase enzymes are not active at these temperatures, however, there is strong evidence that liquefaction of these enzymes is enhanced by a rest at these temperatures, thus preparing the enzyme systems for higher-temperature rests. There is virtually no proteolytic activity in this temperature range, so it is well suited as a low-temperature regime for use with malt that has a high degree of protein modification.

(2) A temperature range of 113–131 °F (45–55 °C) has traditionally been regarded as the regime for protein rests. Here the term is justified. If a gentle, low oxygen pickup mashing system is used,

then a nontrivial amount of protein breakdown will occur. Theoretically, a rest in the 113-122 °F (45-50 °C) range favors the breakdown of medium molecular weight proteins into smaller units, while a rest at 122-131 °F (50-55 °C) favors action on the high molecular weight proteins (de Clerck 1957). In actual mashes and in mathematical simulations, this distinction typically does not exist; and both activities take place, although with a diminished effect, as the temperature is increased. For example, tests show that a rest at 131 °F (55 °C) will not increase the chill-proofing stability over brews that had a protein rest at 122 °F (50 °C) for the same amount of time. However, only trivial amounts of protein degration was seen at 138 °F (59 °C). Glucanase enzymes remain active over the entire range of 113-131 °F (45-55 °C), but this activity sharply decreases with higher temperatures and stops completely at 140 °F (60 °C).

(3) The 140-148 °F (60-64 °C) range has traditionally been regarded as optimal for beta-amylase activity. However, test brews have shown that there is nontrivial beta-amalase activity at temperatures as low as 131 °F (55 °C). In any case, a rest in this range can be used to increase the maltose/maltotriose ratio. More generally, it can be used to increase the RDF.

(4) The range for optimal alpha-amylase activity is 154-162 °F (68-72 °C). Spending the bulk of the time at higher temperatures in this range, as compared to 140-147 °F (60-64 °C), results in lower RDFs than splitting the time equally between the two regimes.

We also can control the amount of oxygen uptake and the amount of hot-side abuse that takes place during mashing. The evidence documenting the negative effects of hot-side aeration is extensive. (For examples see Fix 1992, 15:5; Narziss, *Brauwelt* 1993, 3; Huige 1992.) Of particular relevance to mashing is the need to avoid shearing forces created by excess stirring, as they have a negative impact on enzymatic activity. It was once believed that the traditional protein rest was of limited value, and data were presented to support this conclusion. This was in direct conflict with other data that showed there was significant proteolytic activity during rests at 113-140 °F (45-60 °C). Hot-side aeration was the key in resolving this conflict. In a gentle low oxygen mashing system, protein degradation does take place, but in a less favorable environment, this may not be the case (Uhlig 1992).

Our test brew results illustrate these ideas. We used a 50-liter pilot system, however, the data have been normalized for 1-barrel and 1-hectoliter batches for convenience. A target extract of 12 °P (SG equals 1.048) was selected for the finished wort. Anticipating an approximate 65% yield, we used an equivalent of 50 pounds of malt for the 1-barrel batch and 20 kilograms for the 1-hectoliter batch. The total water used exceeded the batch size by a factor of 1.33, half of which was used in the mash and the other half was used for sparging. On average, there was a 2% loss of extract during sparging, and a 15% loss of moisture. Thus, of the 1.3 hectoliters (1.3 barrels) of water, only 1.1 hectoliters of sweet wort were sent to the kettle. This volume was reduced 10% by evaporation in the boil, giving a final volume near 1 hectoliter (1 barrel).

In some mashing systems, precise temperature control is problematic, which creates a situation where two or more temperature regimes may coexist in the mash at a given rest. In such circumstances, yields, RDFs, and other data can vary in erratic and unpredictable ways. In the test brews cited here, our mash tun was fitted with thermally insulated jackets, and gentle mixing kept the thermal gradients below 2 °F (which is the same as a difference of 1 °C). The data are averages over a number of brews; nevertheless, as temperatures were carefully controlled, variances from batch to batch were under 2%.

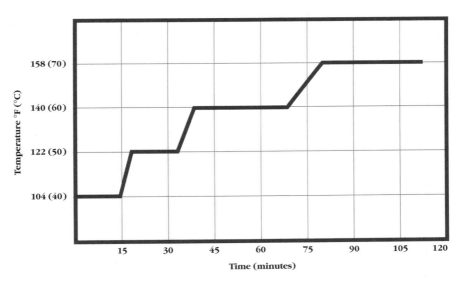

Figure 1.2. The 104-122-140-158 (40-50-60-70) program.

Test Batch Series 1—This series used a European Pilsener malt produced from low protein (10%) two-row barley. It had a moderate degree of protein modification (Kolbach index of 38%) and a high degree of carbohydrate modification (fine/course grind extract difference of 1.7). The best results with this malt came from a mash using all four temperatures cited previously—104, 122, 140, and 158 °F (40, 50, 60, 70 °C). The time and temperature history is shown in figure 1.2.

The malt in test series 1 was doughed-in with 0.5 hectoliter (0.5 barrel) of water at 104 °F (40 °C). After a fifteen-minute hold, another 8 liters (2.6 gallons) of boiling water was added to increase the temperature to 122 °F (50 °C). This was then held for fifteen minutes, after which another 8 liters (2.6 gallons) of boiling water was added. This, plus a small amount of external heat, raised the temperature to 140 °F (60 °C), which was held for thirty minutes. External heat then was used to raise the temperature to 158 °F (70 C°). The final rest was thirty minutes. The results, given in table 1.15, are typical of the data we obtained from this type of system.

Our favorite program with this type of malt omits the rest at 104 °F (40 °C) and spends thirty minutes each at 122 °F (50 °C), 140 °F (60 °C), and 158 °F (70 °C). The 16 liters (5.2 gallons) of extra water can be used to affect the two transitions, so very little if any external heat is required. There is a slight loss of yield (66–67% as opposed to 67–68%), but all other factors remain the same. It is important in a three-temperature program to keep the first rest temperature below 131 °F (55 °C) to ensure good beta-glucanase activity and above 113 °F (45 °C) to ensure good proteolytic activity. A two-temperature program with rests at 140 °F (60 °C) and 158 °F (70 °C) does not lead to satisfactory results. To obtain acceptable yields, the total lautering time needs to be increased significantly with extended recirculation. This ultimately extracts an appropriate amount of grain sugars but also sharply adds to finished beer astringency.

Test Batch Series 2—This series used a low protein (10%), highly modified two-row ale malt. The Kolbach index was 44% and the fine/course grind extract difference was 1.6. The best result with this malt was obtained with a 104-140-158 °F (40-60-70 °C) program, with thirty minutes at each temperature. Since most of the malts available today have Kolbach indices in excess of 40%, the 40-60-70 °C program has become our most frequently used system. Sixteen liters (5.2 gallons) of boiling water were used to increase the temperature from

Table 1.15 Test Batch Series 1 Results

	Variable	1 hL brew	1 bbl. brew
Mash	Volume	0.67 hL	0.67 bbl.
	Percent extract (w/w)	19.2 °P	18.6 °P
	SG	1.079	1.077
	Percent extract (w/v)	20.8 kg/hL	51.9 lbs./bbl.
	Total extract	13.8 kg	34.6 lbs.
	Yield	69%	69%
Sweet Wort	Volume	1.1 hL	1.1 bbl.
	Percent extract (w/w)	11.7 °P	11.4 °P
	SG	1.047	1.046
	Percent extract (w/v)	12.3 kg/hL	30.8 lbs./bbl.
	Total extract	13.5 kg	33.9 lbs.
	Yield	67.5%	67.8%
Finished Wort	Volume	1.0 hL	1.0 bbl.
	Percent extract (w/w)	12.8 °P	12.4 °P
	SG	1.052	1.050
	Maltose/maltotriose	3.4	3.4
	RDF	65%	65%

(1) RDF can be varied by altering the times spent at 140 °F (60 °C) and 158 °F (70 °C). For example, forty-five minutes at the former and fifteen minutes at the latter will generally increase the RDF to the 67–68% range; the reverse will lower it to around 60%.

(2) Sixty minutes at 140 °F (60 °C) or above may be overkill for a malt with a high degree of carbohydrate modification. There are, however, some Pilsener malts that have a much lower degree of carbohydrate modification (with fine/course grind extract differences in excess of 2.0). These malts may require more than sixty minutes to get the same result.

(3) Both the foam quality and chill haze stability of the finished beers were rated as very good. For this type of malt, the 104-122-140-158 (40-50-60-70) program gave sufficient but not excessive protein degradation.

104–140 °F (40–60 °C), and external heat was used for the last transition. Typical data are given in table 1.16.

The comments regarding RDF cited in table 1.15 also apply to this program. One major difference between test series 2 and test series 1 concerns protein modification. Test brews indicate that with highly modified malts, time spent in the 113–131 °F (45–55 °C) temperature range should be kept at a minimum—even a fifteen-minute rest at 122 °F (50 °C) had negative effects. The foam quality was poor, and, even more striking, the underlying malt flavors took on a dull and neutral character. The rest at 104 °F (40 °C), however, proved to

Table 1.16 Test Batch Series 2 Results

	Variable	1 hL brew	1 bbl. brew
Mash	Volume	0.67 hL	0.67 bbl.
	Percent extract (w/w)	19.7 °P	19.1 °P
	SG	1.082	1.079
	Percent extract (w/v)	21.3 kg/hL	53.3 lbs./bbl.
	Total extract	14.2 kg	35.5 lbs.
	Yield	71.0%	71.0%
Sweet Wort	Volume	1.1 hL	1.1 bbl.
	Percent extract (w/w)	12.1 °P	11.7 °P
	SG	1.049	1.047
	Percent extract (w/v)	12.7 kg/hL	31.6 lbs./bbl.
	Total extract	13.9 kg	34.8 lbs.
	Yield	69.5%	69.6%
Finished Wort	Volume	1.0 hL	1.0 bbl.
	Percent extract (w/w)	13.1 °P	12.8 °P
	SG	1.053	1.052
	Maltose/maltotriose	3.5	3.5
	RDF	65%	65%

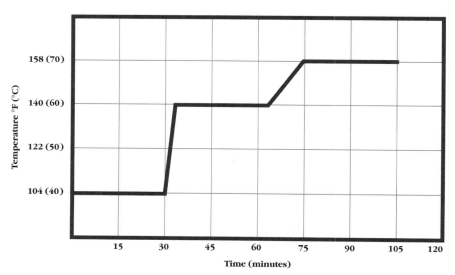

Figure 1.3. The 140-122-158 (40-60-70) program.

be beneficial. The results were much better than with the classic single temperature widely used with ale malts like this one. Figure 1.4 illustrates our test results with the 150 °F (66 °C) program, and data are given in table 1.17.

Omitting the low-temperature rest resulted in a yield loss of nearly 15%. Some brewers compensate for this by using extended recirculation, by extensive lautering, or by crushing the malt into a fine powder. A more preferable option is simply to use more malt. When we tested this, we found little difference between the finished beer quality of a single-temperature mash and a three-temperature mash. However, we want to emphasize that this applies only to low protein, low beta-glucan, and highly modified two-row malts.

Test Batch Series 3—Our final test series used a domestic two-row malt with a relatively high protein content (11.7%), a high degree of protein modification (Kolbach index of 40%), and a moderate degree of carbohydrate modification (fine/course grind extract

Table 1.17 Test Batch 150 (66) Results

	Variable	1 hL brew	1 bbl. brew
Mash	Volume	0.67 hL	0.67 bbl.
	Percent extract (w/w)	17.2 °P	16.6 °P
	SG	1.071	1.068
	Percent extract (w/v)	18.5 kg/hL	46.3 lbs./bbl.
	Total extract	12.3 kg	30.9 lbs.
	Yield	61.5%	61.8%
Sweet Wort	Volume	1.1 hL	1.1 bbl.
	Percent extract (w/w)	10.4 °P	10.2 °P
	SG	1.041	1.040
	Percent extract (w/v)	11.0 kg/hL	27.5 lbs./bbl.
	Total extract	12.1 kg	30.3 lbs.
	Yield	60.5%	60.5%
Finished Wort	Volume	1.0 hL	1.0 bbl.
	Percent extract (w/w)	11.4 °P	11.1 °P
	SG	1.045	1.045
	Maltose/maltotriose	2.9	2.9
	RDF	64%	64%

An Analysis of Brewing Techniques

difference of 2.2). With this malt, we achieved the best results with a 95-131-140-158 °F (35-55-60-70 °C) system. To avoid excess protein degradation, the rest at 122 °F (50 °C) was replaced with a rest at 131 °F (55 °C) and was held for fifteen minutes. The low-temperature rest was taken at 95 °F (35 °C) and was held for thirty minutes. Test results are given in table 1.18.

Some brewers find that their equipment is not suitable for multi-temperature infusion mashing, due primarily to overshoots and large temperature gradients. In such cases, decoction mashing is highly recommended. Darryl Richman's book, *Bock* (1994), describes a well-considered program, easily accommodated with elementary equipment. While it is true that decoction mashing leads to deeper color and to flavor-active constituents not found in infusion mashes, the compounds responsible for these, namely N-heterocyclics, also are generated during wort boiling. We have found that making suitable adjustments in thermal loading during the boil takes care of this (discussed in section Wort Boiling).

Table 1.18 Test Batch Series 3 Results

	Variable	1 hL brew	1 bbl. brew
Mash	Volume	0.67 hL	0.67 bbl.
	Percent extract (w/w)	18.4 °P	17.8 °P
	SG	1.076	1.073
	Percent extract (w/v)	19.8 kg/hL	49.5 lbs./bbl.
	Total extract	13.2 kg	33.0 lbs.
	Yield	66%	66%
Sweet Wort	Volume	1.1 hL	1.1 bbl.
	Percent extract (w/w)	11.2 °P	10.9 °P
	SG	1.045	1.044
	Percent extract (w/v)	11.8 kg/hL	29.4 lbs./bbl.
	Total extract	12.9 kg	32.3 lbs.
	Yield	64.5%	64.6%
Finished Wort	Volume	1.0 hL	1.0 bbl.
	Percent extract (w/w)	12.3 °P	11.9 °P
	SG	1.049	1.048
	Maltose/maltotriose	3.1	3.1
	RDF	66%	66%

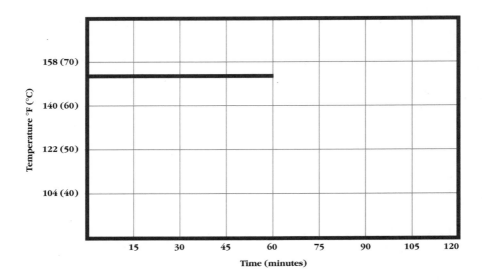

Figure 1.4. The 150 (66) program.

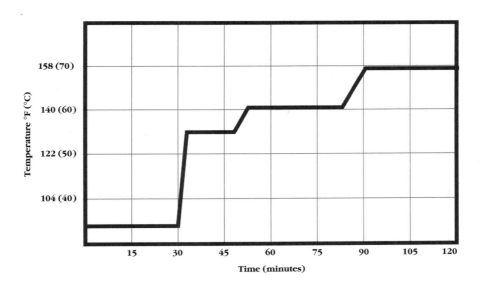

Figure 1.5. The 95-131-140-158 (35-55-60-70) program.

An Analysis of Brewing Techniques

Our test batches illustrate that the optimal mashing system depends very much on the degree of modification of the malt being used. However, it should be noted that in addition to the test batches we have described, there are alternatives that produce nearly optimal results. The crucial points that emerged from our test brews that have wide applicability are:

(1) Mash pH should be kept below 5.5 in order to produce consistent and reproducible results.
(2) If the malt's Kolbach index exceeds 40%, serious consideration should be given to minimizing the time spent in the temperature range of 113–131 °F (45–55 °C).
(3) If the Kolbach index is well below 40%, a rest in the 113–131 °F (45–55 °C) range is advantageous.
(4) In all cases, the inclusion of some type of low-temperature rest (below 113 °F [45 °C]) will increase yields.

HOPS

The constituents of hops, which are dissolved in wort during brewing, are resins, essential oils, sugars, proteins, and tannins. The contributions from the last three are minor compared with what is extracted from malt; consequently, the resins and oils are of greater relevance to brewing. It was traditionally believed that resins are responsible for hop taste, while oils define aroma. Since oils are quite volatile, they are rapidly removed during wort boiling. This led to a distinction between bittering hops, which are added early in the boil for their resin content, and aroma hops, which are added late in the boil for their essential oils. Aroma hops are also sometimes added during beer storage. However, research shows that these are oversimplifications of what actually occurs. For example, when hops are added to beer in storage, both hop aroma and flavor increase, and brewers commonly underestimate the effect late hop additions have on a beer's hop bitterness. In addition, we have found that bittering hops contribute to hop aroma, even when they are added early in the boil. In fact, the more pungent the oil fraction, the greater the effect. Consequently, we believe that all hops should be evaluated by a common standard. In particular, if a bittering hop falls below a brewer's standards with respect to aroma, it should be replaced with one that meets the brewer's expectations—regardless of when it is added in the brewing process.

Resins

Hop resins can be extracted from ground hop cones with methanol and petroleum ether (*ASBC Methods of Analysis* 1992). The following diagram shows how resins are broken down.

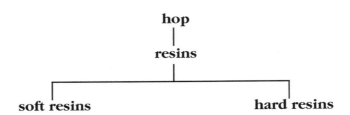

In fresh hops, soft resins dominate, and hard resins typically make up less than 1% of the total resin. As hops age, the hard resins increase and the soft resins decrease, while the total remains essentially constant. Soft resins, which have the greatest relevance to brewing, are made up of alpha acids, beta acids, and gamma acids.

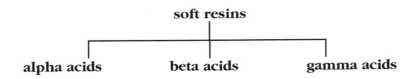

Gamma acids are typically a small percent of the total. They have not been characterized chemically and are believed to be of little importance.

Alpha acids are of greatest relevance because they contribute flavors associated with hop bitterness. Their concentration can be determined by titration with lead acetate (*ASBC Methods of Analysis* 1992) or by photometric methods (Verzeli and de Keukeleire 1991). Alpha acids are only weakly soluble in wort, and during wort boiling they are isomerized into the more soluble iso-alpha-acids. Generally, the total concentration of iso-alpha-acids in wort (or, for that matter, beer) is a good indicator of the intensity of a hop's flavoring, which is measured by a bittering unit (BU) index. Bittering units are measured photometrically (which tends to include a small amount of resins other than iso-alpha-acids) or chromatographically (which is a more specific assay), and they are typically reported in milligrams per liter. Following are some general guidelines:

Hop Bitterness Intensity	BU (mg/L)
Subthreshold	< 10
Low	12–20
Medium	25–35
Strong	> 40

While a beer's BU correlates with the strength of its hop flavor, it does not indicate hop flavor quality. The primary reason for this is that the iso-alpha-acid fractions in beer are treated as equivalents, when in fact they differ chemically and in other ways as well. The major fractions of alpha acids found in hops are:

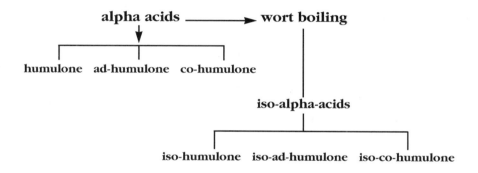

Co-humulone has one less carbon atom than humulone and ad-humulone, which implies that co-humulone has a greater polarity and is more soluble in wort in its isomerized form. Rigby (1972) studied co-humulone and found that the flavoring potential of iso-humulone and iso-ad-humulone tends to be rounded and mellow, while iso-co-humulone tends to impart a crude bitterness. Rigby's results were consistent with the hop varieties in existence at the time of his research; and, indeed, all of the world's most highly valued classic hops have low co-humulone fractions. Nevertheless, his work was criticized by several experts because specific mechanisms linking high co-humulone with harsh bitterness were lacking (Verzeli and de Keukeleire 1991; Wackerbauer and Balzar 1992). A number of new hop varieties have been introduced that shed additional light on the subject.

In particular, it is now clear that a low co-humulone fraction does not necessarily ensure a refined bitter flavor; there are simply too many variables involved. On the other hand, all varieties with high co-humulone have the bitter hop taste Rigby predicted.

Beta acids can be separated into fractions as well:

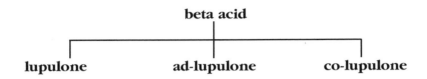

beta acid

lupulone   **ad-lupulone**   **co-lupulone**

In addition, co-lupulone levels, like co-humulone levels, tend to be a varietal characteristic with the classic aroma hops having lower fractions than bittering hops.

The role played by beta acids is not entirely clear. These resins in fresh hops are not readily converted into wort-soluble substances. As hops age, the alpha acid and beta acid levels decrease and oxidize, thus becoming more soluble in wort. Beta acids are included in a larger class of compounds called nonhumulone bitter substances. Wackerbauer identified the following schools of thought (Wackerbauer 1993):

(1) Nonhumulone bitter substances are important and leave a pleasing hoppy taste if the hops have an alpha/beta ratio (a/b) that is sufficiently low. The classic aroma hops satisfy this condition.

a / b = (% alpha acids) / (% beta acids)

(2) Nonhumulone bitter substances are not important.
(3) Nonhumulone bitter substances are important and are the main cause of unpleasant hop flavors.

We did a number of test brews in order to sort out these conflicting viewpoints. Here are our conclusions:

(1) We found the higher the co-humulone percent—a BU in the mid-20s or higher—the cruder the bitter flavor. No conclusion could be drawn when a BU was below 20.

(2) Wort pH is as important (maybe more so) as hop composition. Even fresh, high-quality aroma hops contribute harsh tones in beers wherein the finished wort pH is high.

(3) An important key to controlling wort pH is to establish a proper mash pH. If the latter can be kept below 5.5, the wort pH should finish below 5.3. We found this condition is sufficient to avoid harsh tones.

(4) Nonhumulone bitter substances depend a lot on hop rates. If the BU is below 20, and if aged aroma hops are used, then a rather pleasant hoppiness can be detected that will not be present if hops are fresh. This is consistent with the practice of some large commercial brewers that do not use aroma hops until they are at least one year past harvest. On the other hand, nonhumulone bitter substances do add to beer harshness if aged hops are used in high concentrations. Flavors such as barnlike, cheesy, dank, earthy, grassy, and musty can usually be detected. Thus, at least two schools of thought cited by Wackerbauer may not be conflicting. The validity of either viewpoint depends on the context.

As previously stated, both alpha acids and beta acids decrease as hops age. The extent to which this occurs is difficult to predict accurately since it depends on hop variety, hop type (e.g., cone or pellet), and storage conditions. An added complication is that attenuation of these compounds does not follow first-order kinetics. There are time periods where losses occur at very low rates followed by time periods where the rates are much higher. We found the only reliable way to deal with this issue is to store hops in a cold (preferably below 32 °F [0 °C]), low-oxygen, low-humidity environment. It is also useful to measure the alpha levels of whole hops every four to six months and pellet alpha levels every twelve months.

Essential Oils

The essential oils of hops that are dissolved in beer definitely affect beer aroma and, either directly or indirectly, the overall perception of hop flavor as well. Oil fractions vary significantly with hop variety as well as with the region where hops are grown. Often, the total oil content of a hop is quoted, but this is not nearly as important as the oil fractions present in a hop. Therefore, our analysis concentrates on the latter.

Essential oil composition can be broadly classified as:

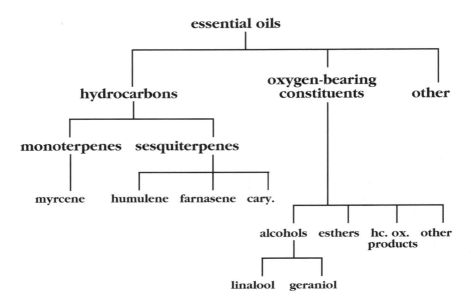

Hydrocarbons and oxygen-bearing constituents are the most relevant to beer, although sometimes sulfur-bearing constituents resulting from heavy pesticide use have been isolated in both hops and the beer brewed from them. Hydrocarbons are made up of monoterpene and sesquiterpene. Monoterpene is essentially myrcene, a compound that has an extremely crude and unpleasant aroma. The major sesquiterpene fractions are humulene, farnasene, and caryophylene. Sesquiterpene has a refined and elegant smell. For this reason, the sesquiterpene/monoterpene (s/m) ratio is important:

s / m = (total sesquiterpenes – mL/kg) / (total monoterpenes – mL/kg).

However, the sesquiterpene/monoterpene ratio should be used carefully because farnasene is difficult to measure accurately, even with chromography.

Linalool is the major hop alcohol found in virtually all beers. In isolation it has a distinct, floral/hoppy smell that is valued by those who like beer. Geraniol is another alcohol with floral tones, but in isolation, it has other tones that recall cheap, rank perfume.

Many ester fractions have been identified, but their effects are difficult to characterize. There is some evidence that hop esters are

An Analysis of Brewing Techniques

responsible for some of the unique aromas of selected varieties. Therefore, it is interesting that all the classic aroma hops have very low total ester levels, which is why the ester/oxygen-bearing component (e/obc) ratio is important:

$$e / obc = (total\ esters - mL/kg) / (total\ oxygen\text{-}bearing\ components - mL/kg).$$

Oxidation products of humulene, such as humulene epoxides, humulenol, and humuladienone, play an important role in aged-hop aroma. In isolation, these compounds have a grassy and haylike smell that is easy to distinguish from the cheesy and valeric tones of oxidized resins.

Hop Varieties

In applying these ideas to the major hop varieties available today, it is convenient to group hops with similar quality ratios (see tables 1.19–1.23). Our grouping method was strongly influenced by the work of Peacock (1992), Foster and Schmidt (1994), and Haunold and Nickerson (1993).

All of the quality factors of classic aroma hops (table 1.19) fall into the excellent category, which is probably why these hops are valued by brewers the world over for their refined taste and aroma. Subgroups in table 1.19 are differentiated by their characteristics; for example, German hops tend to fall in the lower range while U.S. and

Table 1.19 Group I: Classic Aroma Hops

Hop Variety
(a)   German Hallertau, German Hersbrucker
(b)   German Tettnanger, Czechoslavakian Saaz, German Spalter
(c)   U.K. East Kent Goldings
(d)   U.K. and Slovenian Styrian Goldings, U.K. Fuggles, U.S. Willamettes

Characteristics
(i)   Low to average alpha levels: 3–6.5%
(ii)   Low co-humulone fractions: 20–25%
(iii) Low a/b ratios: 0.8–1.2
(iv)   High s/m ratios: 2.5–4
(v)   Low e/obc ratios

U.K. hops tend to be in the upper range. Saaz-type hops tend to have high farnasene levels, and this is widely felt to be the reason for their special aroma. (It should be noted that farnasene is virtually destroyed in the pelletizing process, so the aroma is best seen in whole hops.) Farnasene is also present in Hallertau-type hops, *(a)*, but at very low levels; *(c)* and *(d)* have mid-range farnasene levels. The linalool level of all five subgroups is high, but *(d)* has very high levels.

Table 1.20 Group II: Special Hops

Hop Variety
(a)   U.S. Cascade
(b)   German and U.S. Northern Brewer, German and U.S. Perle
Characteristics
(i)   Average alpha levels: 6–9%
(ii)   Average co-humulone fractions: 25–30%
(iii) Average a/b ratios: 1.8–2.5
(iv) Average s/m ratios: 1.1–1.8
(v)   High e/obc ratios

The special characteristics of group II hops are what distinguish them (table 1.20). Cascade, which is open-pollinated with Fuggles and the Russian Serebrianka, has very high levels of both linalool and geraniol. This combination gives a unique and unmistakable fruity/hoppy/floral taste and smell that usually recalls grapefruit. Northern Brewer has very high linalool levels but low geraniol levels. This is why Northern Brewer tends to have a wider application than Cascade for imparting a hoppy taste to beer as an early-addition bittering hop. Cascade, however, has been very successful in U.S. ale styles, and, indeed, a strong case can be made that the floral hop taste is a key difference between U.S. and U.K. ales. Perle comes closest to group I hops, except that its quality parameters differ from group I hops by 15–30%.

Subgroup *(b)* of group III (table 1.21) consists of transplants of genetically unaltered hops cultivated in the United States, *(a)* and *(c)* consist of new varieties that have a large fraction of "noble-type" hops in their parentage (Haunold and Nickerson 1990). All of these hops are seen as potential competitors and replacements for the German hops in group *(a)* and *(b)*. Their quality indices are close to those of "noble-type" hops, particularly in the crucial areas of percent co-humulone and sesquiterpene/monoterpene ratio. It is our opinion that despite their high-brewing quality, these hops are best taken on their own terms and not seen as replacements. For example, U.S. Tettanger hops are quite different from their German counterparts and, for example, have a much *lower* farnasene content. Mt. Hood, a Hallertau clone, has a much higher farnasene content than the latter, while Liberty, another Hallertau clone, does not. Ultra, one of the newest varieties, comes the closest to the classic Hallertau profile, and many people think it will emerge as the best of the group III varieties. Crystal, on the other hand, is unique among the group III hops. It has a taste and smell that is definitely European, but it tends to be more intensely hoppy than the others in this group. Like Ultra, Crystal is also finding wide acceptance, particularly with craft brewers.

Table 1.21 Group III: U.S. Versions of "Noble-Type" Hops

Hop Variety	
(a)	Ultra, Crystal
(b)	Hallertau, Tettanger
(c)	Liberty, Mt. Hood
Characteristics	
(i)	low to average alpha levels: 3–5%
(ii)	low cohumulone fractions: 20–25%
(iii)	low a/b ratios: 0.8–1.2
(iv)	high s/m ratios: 2.5–4
(v)	low e/obc ratios

Subgroups *(a)* and *(b)* in table 1.22 have the lowest co-humulone percentages, typically near 30%. We found that Olympic has a harsh but thin bitterness that leaves a lingering aftertaste, and Nugget has strange herbal undertones that wash out rather quickly. The aroma associated with both these hops has crude tones. Columbus, a new high alpha variety, is strikingly different in that it produces a big but rather mellow bitterness. Its total oil content is high and it has a pleasant aroma. Its cohumulone and s/m ratios are much closer to the noble hops (group I) than any of the other hops in group III. To our palates, all the hops in subgroup *(c)* have a harsh and clinging bitterness and a strong and pungent aroma.

Wort Production

Table 1.22 Group IV: U.S. High-Alpha Level Hops

Hop Variety	
(a)	Columbus
(b)	Nugget, Olympic
(c)	Centennial, Chinook, Eroica, Galena
Characteristics	
(i)	High alpha levels: 10–14%
(ii)	High co-humulone fractions: 30–40%
(iii)	High a/b ratios: 2.5–3
(iv)	Low s/m ratios: < 1
(v)	High e/obc ratios

Table 1.23 Group V: Moderate Alpha Bittering Hops

Hop Variety	
(a)	U.S. Cluster
(b)	German Brewer's Gold
Characteristics	
(i)	Average alpha levels: 6–8%
(ii)	Extremely high co-humulone fractions: 35–40%
(iii)	High a/b ratios: 2.5–3
(iv)	Low s/m ratios: < 1
(v)	Very high e/obc ratios

Cluster is the most important U.S. hop from a historical perspective. New York was for a long time the most important hop growing region in the country, and the literature suggests that Cluster has always been the dominant hop variety (Hind 1950; Neve 1991). As hop cultivation shifted westward, first to California and then to the Pacific Northwest, Cluster remained the dominant variety. Today, it is ranked in the top three in terms of acreage, although this is somewhat deceptive since the bulk of the crop goes into various hop extracts, wherein varietal characteristics do not play an important role. Cluster has a very strong aroma that typically recalls black currents. Many English authors have dubbed it the "American Aroma" or, less flattering, the "Tom Cat smell."

Brewer's Gold was originally developed in England by Solman as a hybrid of U.S. and U.K. hops. Ironically, today it is primarily grown in Hallertau, but the majority is exported. It, along with Cluster, has the most unfavorable quality index of any of the varieties discussed so far. In addition, both have extremely high geraniol levels, which, along with their elevated myrcene levels, possibly explains their crude taste and smell. Cluster was primarily used by regional breweries in the 1950s and 1960s. Many feel that the image that developed during this period—that national beers were of higher quality than local brews—was in large part due to the fact that national brewers used higher quality brewing materials and, in particular, higher quality hops. In any case, we think the trend toward lower hop rates in regional beers was due to Cluster, as its effects diminish sharply as the concentration decreases.

The hop varieties cited in tables 1.19–1.23 are not the only ones of interest to brewers; rather, they are the ones we have had direct practical brewing experience with. Following are additional varieties, broken down geographically.

Australia—Pride of Ringwood is Australia's traditional hop. It is said to be similar to Cluster in character.

Germany—New aroma varieties include Hallertau Traditional, Hallertau Huller, and Spalt Select. All have received high marks in trial brews, and their futures appear bright. A new high alpha variety, Hallertau Magnum, is also being bred as a replacement for Brewer's Gold.

New Zealand—Due to its favorable geographic location, New Zealand is emerging as one of the world's most important hop-growing areas. The diseases that have ravaged sections of Hallertau, the Kent district in the United Kingdom, and elsewhere are unknown in New Zealand. Because of this the use of potentially flavor-destructive pesticide is minimal or nonexistent. Moreover, recent years have seen plantings of the classic hop varieties like Saaz and Hallertau. These are just starting to become available to brewers in the United States, but results from test brews have been very promising. Sicklebract and Green Bullett, varieties native to New Zealand, are quite different. They tend to have an unique earthy taste and smell that falls very much into the "love it or leave it" category.

Poland—Lublin, Poland's traditional variety, has received high marks as an aroma hop. It is a Saaz-type hop, but with earthy tones not seen in spicy Czechoslovakian hops or in German Tettnanger. The largest brewer in the United States uses this variety as part of an aroma blend.

United Kingdom—In recent years, a number of new hop varieties have been introduced in the United Kindom. One of the most exciting is First Gold, which is a commercial dwarf variety. Its aroma characteristics are very close to Goldings. Our trial brews with this hop were highly favorable. Brambling Cross and Progress have also been proposed as Goldings replacements. A number of medium to high alpha and high co-humulone varieties have also been introduced, including Herald (another dwarf), Phoenix, and Pioneer. These join Omega, Target, and Yeoman, which have similar characteristics.

United States—Turn-of-the-century Budweiser labels have Saaz hops listed on them, and brewers have long had an interest in growing this hop in the United States. Although early efforts failed, the current program appears to be gathering momentum. In 1994 some domestically grown Saaz hops became available on the commercial market, and in the future, more may be seen.

Most of the varieties we have discussed are grown seedless. This is because the oil from the seeds is potentially foam negative and can take on rancid flavors when oxidized (Zattler and Krauss 1970). Continental lager brewers have been particularly resistive to seeded hops, and they are explicitly banned in Germany. The only reason hops are grown seeded is based on economics. Male and female plants are grown separately; thus, if male plants are contiguous to female plants, the latter will pollinate and produce seeds. The net effect is to fertilize the female plants and increase yields. Today, seeded hops are grown only in the United Kingdom and in Willamette valley of Oregon. Even in these regions, it is only older varieties like East Kent Goldings, Fuggles, and Styrian Goldings that are grown seeded. This favorable change is primarily due to genetic engineering (Haunold 1974).

WORT BOILING

When wort is boiled the following physical and chemical changes take place:

- Coagulable proteins are excreted
- pH drops due to calcium and wort phosphate reactions

- Enzymes and foreign microbes are destroyed
- Wort volume is reduced by evaporation
- Wort gravity is proportionally increased

In addition, there are four other activities that can and should be controlled by brewers:

- Hop additions
- Hop extraction
- Dimethyl sulfide (DMS) reduction
- Maillard reactions

Hop Additions

In modern brewing, one or more of the following methods are typically used:

(1) Hops are added near the beginning or in the middle of the boil. Contact times range from thirty to sixty minutes.
(2) Hops are added near the end of the boil or just after the boil has been completed (late hopping).
(3) Hops are added on the cold side during the maturation of beer (dry hopping).

De Clerck compared (1) and (2) and then strongly recommended (1) (de Clerck 1957). He found late-kettle hopping to be wasteful at best, and harmful to beer flavor at worse. Modern chromatography supports de Clerck's theory that the first method is best (Mitter 1995; Preis and Mitter 1995). While hop oil constituents are highly volatile as isolated compounds, chromatographs show that during kettle boiling many get bound up with wort constituents at concentrations much higher than anticipated. Moreover, many of these hop oil constituents are stable and can be detected in finished beer. This justifies de Clerck's assertion that "beer will always retain the smell of hops no matter when they are added" (de Clerck 1959).

Late hopping is quite different. Chromatography shows that late hopping tends to add to the iso-co-humulone content of beer, even with high-quality, low co-humulone hops. Given the polarity and solubility of co-humulone, this is not surprising, and it is also consistent with de Clerck's concern that late hopping contributes a harsher bitter. The hop oil constituent levels of worts produced using late hopping tend to be higher, but this is not seen in the finished beer. This means that the aroma compounds produced using late hopping are unstable (i.e., only weakly bound up in beer) and will disappear before the beer is packaged. Again, de Clerck's theory remains intact.

The third method, post-fermentation hopping, or dry hopping, is a good deal more complicated. The alcohol that is present extracts the resins. However, none of the humulone fractions are favored, and, in particular, the co-humulone fraction extracted is representative of what is present in the hop used. Indeed, studies comparing dry hopping with late-kettle hopping using premium hops have consistently favored the former (Fix, *Principles of Brewing Science* 1989). The real issue with dry hopping is stability, not quality. In England, where dry-hopped, cask-conditioned ales are consumed twenty-four to thirty-six hours after they have reached proper carbonation levels, stability is not a big issue. In this context, dry hopping is almost universally accepted. However dry hopping is not favored by continental European brewers, most likely due to the prevalence of bottled beer as well as keg beer that is protected under carbon dioxide pressure. Carbon dioxide tends to prevent the oxidative deterioration of beer flavors and of hop aroma constituents, however, it also tends to mask/remove these constituents. De Clerck was right in the sense that the first method and the type of hops used will by and large define the finished beer's aroma.

Recently, several German brewers have reintroduced first-wort hopping into their process (Miller 1995; Preis and Mitter 1995). This is an old practice where hops are added to the brew kettle just before it is filled (Wiegmann 1912; Zimmermann 1904). De Clerck's theory suggests that such a practice is reasonable, and, indeed, he proposed a closely related procedure where hops are steeped in water before being added to the boiling wort. Organoleptic analysis suggests that for German Pilsener beer, first-wort hopping gives a much better hop flavor (i.e., taste and smell) than either middle hopping or late hopping (Preis and Mitter 1995). Of particular interest are the chromatographics of hop oil constituents. The total amount of oils in packaged beer did not differ in first-wort hopping compared to alternatives; however, the type of oils that were present were strikingly different. On the other hand, there was a discernible improvement in the quality of taste and smell from first-wort hopping.

Test brews of German Pilseners and Dortmunders brewed with first-wort hopping were entered in ten major competitions from

October 1996 through December 1996. Every entry won an award, and the malt/hop profile was most often cited as the most desirable feature of the beer. To what extent first-wort hopping can be used in other beer styles remains an open question. Of particular interest would be a careful study comparing first-wort hopping with dry hopping for pale ales, India pale ales, and other ales having a big hop profile.

Our own test brews have indicated that a combined procedure may have advantages. We steam dry hops for fifteen minutes before adding to beer maturation tanks. This preprocessing did seem to favorably effect the stability and roundness of the hop taste and smell. On the other hand, the overall intensity of the beer's taste and smell was comparable to that of standard dry hopping without the preprocessing step.

Hop Extraction

The two key parameters of hop extraction are the alpha levels of the hops and the kettle utilization rate (KUR). The latter is defined by the following:

KUR = [(iso-alpha-acids dissolved) / (alpha acids added)] x 100.

It is customary to express both the alpha and iso-alpha levels in milligrams per liter, and we will use BU as the total amount of iso-alpha-acids dissolved in milligrams per liter. Letting AA denote the total amount of alpha acids added, it follows from the kettle utilization rate equation that

BU = KUR x AA / 100.

When multiple additions of hops are used, each will typically have its own kettle utilization rate, and in such cases, the total BU is the sum of the BUs associated with each addition. In general, kettle utilization rate depends on the following:

- Hop type (whole, pellet, or extract)
- Contact time
- Temperature and pressure of the boiling wort
- Wort gravity
- Hop variety
- Hop concentration
- Equipment used (kettle geometry, heating surfaces, etc.)

There are a number of rules that have been proposed for approximating the kettle utilization rate (*Zymurgy* 1990), but we found these rules can err by as much as 25%. Even so, they are not without practical value. For example, while the values of the calculated BU may be way off the mark, marginal adjustments to the hop rates based on the calculations may be far more accurate. This type of analysis can be improved by estimating the kettle utilization rate based on direct BU measurement of liter-sized test brews. Such approximations do not take into account hop variety, hop concentration, or the equipment used, but they do accurately reflect hop type, contact time, temperature and pressure, and wort gravity.

Table 1.24 KUR Estimation

Wort gravity: 12 °P (1.048)	
Post-boil hot wort contact time: 20 minutes	
Hop type: whole	
Volume reduction: 10%	
Boil Time (minutes)	**KUR (percent)**
First wort	30 ± 1.0
60	26 ± 0.5
45	24 ± 0.5
30	20 ± 1.0
15	10 ± 1.0

We want to emphasize that the data in table 1.24 are valid only for the conditions cited. For example, the rates obtained for hop pellets are underestimated, and the rates for high-gravity worts are overestimated (say greater than 14 °P). Moreover, post-boil contact time is very important, and kettle utilization rates at one- to fifteen-minute boil times are strongly influenced by the length of post-boil contact.

Table 1.25 contains a specific example using the BUs from table 1.24. These calculations predict a dissolved iso-alpha concentration of 3.17 grams per hectoliter, which is the same as a BU of 31.7 milligrams per liter. Actual measurements of wort BUs done on our 50-liter pilot system fall in the range of 29–35 milligrams per liter. This is typical of what we found for empirically derived kettle utilization rates: they will not be exact, and using them will lead to errors in the 10% or less range.

Table 1.25 Test Brew

| Initial volume: 1.1 hL |
| Final volume: 1.0 hL |
| Boil time: 90 mins. |
| Initial gravity: 10.8 °P (1.043) |
| Final gravity: 12 °P (1.048) |

Hop addition	Contact time	Alpha (%)	Hop weight (g)	AA (g/hL)	KUR (%)	Added iso-alpha (g/hL)
1	60	8.2	85	6.97	25	1.74
2	30	4.5	145	6.53	20	1.31
3	0	3.8	60	2.28	5	0.12
						3.17

The BU of a finished beer will generally be lower than that of chilled wort. Losses come from three different areas. The first occurs during fermentation. A fraction of the wort's iso-alpha-acid pool will be entrained in the yeast sediment at the bottom of the fermenter. Measurements indicate this can run from 10–20% of the total (Garetz 1994). The second loss occurs during storage. Iso-alpha loss in storage can occur by the same mechanism as in fermentation, however, the extent of the loss is typically much less than during fermentation. If post-fermentation hopping (dry hopping) is used, measurements indicate that the BU will generally increase, though to what extent is hard to predict. It is likely that some form of ethanol extraction is involved but the mechanisms are unclear. The third BU loss occurs during filtration (see Filtration in chapter 5).

Unfortunately, current methodology does not permit a complete quantification of hop oil extraction. Direct measurement using gas chromatography is the only option available. Clearly, this is an area where more research is needed, both for oil extraction and evaporation during wort boiling and for extraction during post-fermentation.

Dimethyl Sulfide Reduction

Another important task of wort boiling is to reduce the sulfur constituents to appropriate levels. Many compounds are relevant (Fix 1992, 15:3), but the one typically monitored is dimethyl sulfide (DMS). There are two reasons DMS is singled out: (1) DMS is an important part of beer flavor in its own right, particularly as a key flavor discriminator between ales and lagers; and (2) the fate of DMS in the boil is shared by the other sulfur compounds, so it serves as a useful tracer compound.

The flavor threshold of DMS is around 30 micrograms per liter. Most ales have DMS levels well below threshold, and any type of sulfur flavor in these beers is widely regarded as a serious technical flaw. Medium- to high-gravity continental pale lagers, on the other hand, have DMS values anywhere from one and one-half to three times threshold. The same is true of some regional U.S. lagers (typically those from the Midwest), although the nature of these flavors is quite different because of the malts used. There is a general trend, both on the Continent and in the United States, to reduce DMS levels in lagers and to keep them below threshold in low-gravity and average-gravity beers.

The most relevant DMS precursor found in malt is S-methyl methionine (SMM), but malt types differ a great deal in their S-methyl methionine content. For example, pale ale malts contain 1–2 micrograms of S-methyl methionine per gram of malt, while many lager malts contain 8–10.

S-methyl methionine is broken down to DMS under heat, according to first-order kinetics. Figure 1.6 is a time history of the attenuation of SMM at various temperatures. For example, suppose we use 20 kilograms of lager malt for a 1-hectoliter brew, and the average S-methyl methionine content is 5 micrograms per gram. This means that at the start of the boil there will be approximately 20 x 5 x 10 = 1,000 ppb of S-methyl methionine dissolved in the wort, and S-methyl methionine will be broken down into DMS (according to the equation in figure 1.6). Therefore, if a ninety-minute boil at 212 °F (100 °C) is used, only 21% of the S-methyl methionine will survive the boil. If proper ventilation is used, the DMS formed will be expelled with kettle exhaust. This means that at the start of cooling, the wort will not contain any DMS and 1,000 x 0.21 = 210 ppb of S-methyl methionine. (Here ppb = parts per billion = micrograms per liter.) Suppose we cool the wort down from 212 °F (100 °C) to 50 °F (10 °C) in sixty minutes. Using an average temperature of (212 + 50) / 2 = 131 °F ([100 + 10] / 2 = 55 °C), figure 1.6 suggests that 53% of the S-methyl methionine will survive cooling. If this is done in a closed system, the remaining 47% will be converted to DMS that will be dissolved in wort. In particular, the chilled wort will contain 210 x 0.47 = 98.7 ppb of DMS, which is approximately three times its threshold. There will be some reduction in DMS during the fermentation, but this rarely exceeds 25% of the total. Thus, the finished beer in this particular case will have a high sulfur profile.

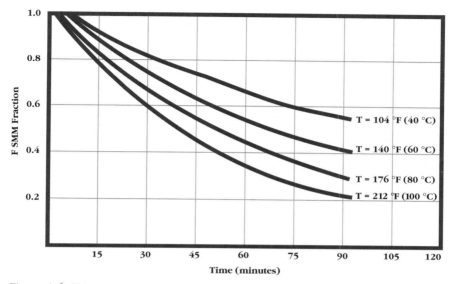

Figure 1.6. SMM to DMS conversion curve. Curves are well approximated by the relation: F = exp (-t × T × 1nZ / 400). (F = % SMM present; t = time; T = temperature °F [°C].)

Corrective action can be taken, such as reducing the cooling time. For example, if the cooling time in the above example is cut in half, to thirty minutes, then the dissolved DMS level will drop from 99 to 59 ppb. Also, holding the worts just under 212 °F (100 °C) for fifteen minutes after the boil is another way to achieve low DMS levels. Using the same calculations for an ale malt with an S-methyl methionine content in the 1–2 microgram per liter range shows that DMS will be at subthreshold levels no matter what type of cooling procedure is used.

Another procedure that is gaining commercial acceptance is "dusting" the wort with nitrogen (air with the oxygen fraction removed) during cooling, which typically reduces DMS levels to well below threshold (Taylor et al. 1982).

Dimethyl sulfide can also be created by bacterial infections, with gram-negative wort spoilers being a particular threat. These bacteria die off early in fermentation, but they can create copious amounts of DMS before that happens. Less common but no less dangerous are anaerobic gram negative bacteria, like *Pectinatus*, that can create DMS during beer storage. Dimethyl sulfide derived from either of these sources tends to have an unmistakable rotten vegetable/cooked corn tone.

Maillard Reactions

Research into the origin of desirable and undesirable malt flavors has identified select heterocyclic compounds formed from Maillard reactions that have a fundamental impact on the quality of a beer's malt flavors (Narziss, *Brauwelt* 1992, 4). Maillard reactions, often called nonenzymatic browning, are interactions between carbohydrates and amino acids (Fix, *Principles of Brewing Science* 1989). As far as brewing is concerned, the heat-induced Maillard reactions are the most relevant. These reactions take place during the malt kiln and mashing. However, it is during wort boiling where the ultimate fate of these compounds is determined. It is convenient to classify Maillard compounds as simple melanoidins, sulfur-bearing heterocyclic compounds, and indicator substances for off-flavors in beer.

Simple Melanoidins—These compounds are typically derived from nonroasted malts (table 1.7). Sweet wort produced from these malts and from decoction mashes are typically rich in simple melanoidins. If passed on to the finished beer, they tend to give a fine malt/malty flavor, generally regarded as favorable in a wide range of beer styles. Excessive thermal loading during the wort boiling (e.g., long boil times or high-temperature/high-pressure boils) can transform simple melanoidins into less desirable heterocyclic compounds.

Sulfur-Bearing Heterocyclic Compounds—These products are found in a number of different foods that have been subjected to high thermal environments (Heath 1988). The desirability of heterocyclics depends on the beer style in question; if they play a minor role in flavor tone, they can be acceptable, otherwise not. A class often found in beer consists of polymers wherein simple melanoidins have complexed with methionines. In finished beer, these compounds have unmistakable vegetal malt tones, which at too high a level are even more unpleasant than DMS. Table 1.26 lists additional sulfur-bearing heterocyclic compounds we consider relevant.

Indicator Substances for Off-Flavors in Beer—These compounds are generally regarded as totally incompatible with beer. Descriptors like bready/worty, burnt caramel, and tobacco smoke have been used to describe the resulting flavors. Unfortunately the offending compounds have not been characterized. However, research has identified indicator substances which are not actually responsible for the off flavors, but their presence in beer coincides with the presence of off flavors. Moreover, extreme thermal loading of wort appears to be the most likely mechanism of their creation

An Analysis of Brewing Techniques

Table 1.26 Sulfur-Bearing Heterocyclic Compounds

Structure	Name	Sensory Property
	2-Methyl-4-propyl-1, 3-exathiane	Fruity, green, slightly burnt
	3H-1, 2-dithiole	Cooked asparagus
	2-Acetyl-2-thiazoline	Freshly baked bread
	Benzothiazole	Quinolinelike, rubbery odor
	1, 2, 4 Trithiolane	Sulfurous
	N-Methyl-thiazolidine	Green coconut
	Sugar/methionine products	Cooked cabbage

(Narziss, *Brauwelt* 1992, 4). Inferior roasted malts are also suspected to be culprits.

The key to successful wort boiling is to avoid excess and to find a balance. Extracting hop constituents and removing DMS require at least some thermal loading. We found that percent of volume evaporation during the boil is a very useful control parameter. Here are some useful guidelines:

(1) The best general recommendation is an evaporation rate of 9–11%. This can usually be achieved with a ninety-minute boil.
(2) If decoction mashing is used for a beer style normally produced by infusion mashing (e.g., British-style ales), keep the evaporation rate in the range of 6–7%.
(3) If infusion mashing is used for a beer style normally produced by a decoction mash (e.g., bock), an evaporation rate as high as 12–14% is advantageous.
(4) In all cases, avoid evaporation rates in excess of 15%.

On several occasions we have seen experienced tasters incorrectly identify the mashing method used when the thermal loading in the boil was adjusted according to (2) and (3). Also striking is the number of times the negative effects from (4) are incorrectly identified as problems in fermentation.

2

Yeast

STRAINS

Each yeast strain has its own personality and characteristic flavor signature, which is why yeast strain selection is the most important step in developing a successful beer formulation. Fortunately, there are a large number of strains available as well as a number of suppliers. This section provides an overview of the more important options.

A systematic yeast strain classification system relevant to brewing is difficult to provide because changes can occur in yeast samples, either during maintenance by the supplier or during brewing. A good case in point is provided by Poirier and Lang (1978). Their brewery, a medium-sized regional in New York, used the same lager strain for years, purchased from a single supplier. Occasional off-flavor nuances—particularly in their delicately flavored beers—suggested that the pitching yeast may not have been a pure culture. Additional analysis done by consultants revealed that at least six strains were present. Table 2.1 shows the individual flavor profiles they found in the Christian Schmidt strain Poirier and Lang were using.

It has been our experience that (1) is the closest to the original culture and the most pure version. The elevated diacetyl levels reported with (4), (5), and (6) indicate they are very likely respiratory-deficient mutants—the fault of the brewery and not the supplier. Strains (2) and (3) are likely the result of the supplier's maintenance procedures. Skews in the overall beer flavor profile produced by (3) are not uncommon.

Because of these and other related examples, we decided to take a strictly functional approach to yeast classification, characterizing

Table 2.1 Substrains of Christian Schmidt

Strain	Flavor Profile
Original mixed culture	Clean, fruity/estery, appreciably sulfury
1	Clean, very beery, good ester-sulfur balance
2	Clean, estery, slightly sulfury
3	Mercaptan flavor, very unpleasant
4	Diacetyl odor, very unpleasant
5	Strongly diacetyl, slightly sulfury
6	Diacetyl odor, flavors are okay

various strains on the basis of the pure versions' behaviors. Any specific version from a specific supplier may or may not share the characteristics described, depending on the purity of the sample.

Functional Attributes

Flavor Profiles—Under normal circumstances, each strain displays its own propensity for creating and/or reducing fermentation products, such as esters, fusel alcohols, diacetyl, and sulfur compounds. By and large, this defines the flavor signature of each strain in its pure form.

Preferred Temperature and Environmental Conditions—Each strain has a preferred fermentation temperature for optimal behavior. Other important issues are alcohol tolerance, oxygen demand, and sensitivity to wort composition.

Apparent Attenuation—Most brewing strains fully metabolize monosaccharides and disaccharides, however, the ability to metabolize trisaccharides and trace sugars varies. This effect is captured by a method called apparent attenuation. Apparent attenuation is the percent drop in apparent extract (i.e., as measured by a hydrometer without alcohol corrections) that is typically achieved by the strain under normal circumstances.

Flocculation—There are significant differences in the flocculation characteristics of brewing strains, ranging from highly flocculant, to powdery, to nonflocculant. The exact mechanism that induces flocculation is poorly understood, but it is known to be a genetic characteristic that can change with mutation (Russel 1995).

Stability—Mutations in pure yeast cultures are usually induced by unfavorable environmental conditions. Examples include elevated temperatures, osmotic stress due to high ethanol levels, and starvation due to lack of nutrients. Nevertheless, each strain tends to display its own propensity toward mutation, with some strains being more forgiving of adverse environments.

The following are sources of the yeast we used in our evaluations:

(1) Siebel Institute of Technology
     4055 W. Peterson Ave.
     Chicago, Illinois 60646-6001

(2) Wyeast Laboratories
     PO Box 425
     Mount Hood, Oregon 97041

(3) Hefebank Weihenstephan
     8050 Feising 12
     Germany

(4) Food Research Institute
     Colony Lane
     Norwich, United Kingdom NR4 7UA

(5) Brewers Resource (BrewTech yeast strains)
     PO Box 507
     Woodland Hills, California 91365

(6) Yeast Labs
     1308 W. Madison
     Ann Arbor, Michigan 48103

(7) White Labs
     7955 Silvertone Ave.
     San Diego, California 92126

The above list is by no means a complete set of yeast suppliers. Our goal was not to test all strains available from all suppliers, but rather limit our study to the major strains in their pure form. We have found the yeast strains listed to be reliable, but this is not to suggest that alternates not on the list are not also reliable.

Lager Yeast

Genetic research of yeast strains has centered around chromosome fingerprinting as a biological discriminator (Casey 1996). Studies show there is considerable heterogeneity in the chromosomes of ale and wheat beer yeast. However, the fingerprints of lager yeast were closely related, indicating a strong similarity to the pure culture introduced in 1883 by Hansen (Raines, *Yeast Culturing* 1992). The group 1 classification is consistent with the homogeneity of lager yeast. In practical terms, we found that today there are only two functionally different versions—malty and dry/crisp. Group 1 yeast is the latter, group 2 yeast the former.

Group 1—These strains typically produce beers with a crisp, clean, and refreshingly dry finish. Under normal conditions, diacetyl, ester, and sulfur levels are well below threshold. As a consequence, this group is preferred for American and Scandinavian-style lagers as well as German-style Pilseners.

Versions: American/St. Louis and North German
- Optimal temperature: 50–54 °F (10–12 °C)
- Apparent attenuation: 75–78%
- Flocculation: Slightly powdery
- Stability: Good during first five to six generations

American/St. Louis lager yeast is a product of one of the world's largest brewing companies. Beer produced with this yeast tends to have a refreshingly snappy finish that recalls apples. Many feel this flavor is a consequence of brewing procedures (kraeusening with a rather brief twenty-one-day cycle time), and not an intrinsic part of the strain's flavor signature. Sources and order numbers: BrewTech CL-620, Wyeast 2007, White Labs WLP020, and Yeast Lab L34.

North German lager yeast comes from a brewery in northern Germany that is well known for its clean, crisp, and hoppy Pilseners. Source and order number: BrewTech CL-660.

Group 2—These strains leave a full and rounded flavor that complements the malt. Typically, there is a subtle sulfur residual, but this normally has a clean malt character. Group 2 strains tend to be very sensitive to the wort's amino acid pool and have a tendency to misbehave if it falls much below 200 milligrams per liter. Thus, they work best with all-malt beers or high-gravity adjunct beers. As a rule, all versions display good alcohol tolerance. Group 2 strains are almost universally used in Bavaria for both pale and dark beers. We believe they are quite appropriate for amber lagers as well. On a historical note, these strains traditionally found acceptance in regional breweries in the Midwest; and, along with midwestern six-row barley, they gave definition to the unique character of those beers.

Versions: W-34/70, W-206, W-308, Christian Schmidt, and California Steam

- Optimal temperature: 45–50 °F (7–10 °C)
- Apparent attentuation: 78–82%
- Flocculation: Good
- Stability: Good

The W-34/70 yeast strain is now the most widely used lager yeast in Germany and has found acceptance in the United States as well (Donhauser et al. 1988). Sources and order names: Weihenstephan W-34/70, Wyeast 2278, and Yeast Lab L31.

The strain W-206 has found wide acceptance in Europe. It is similar in character to W-34/70, except it tends to have slightly higher ester levels. (We suspect it is very close to strain (2) in table 2.1.) Sources and order numbers: Weihenstephan W-206, Wyeast 2206, Siebel BRY-206, and Yeast Labs L32.

The strain W-308 was once widely used in Germany but has all but disappeared there. The major complaint is its tendency to become unstable when reused in practical brewing situations. We feel it is very close to Christian Schmidt and to strain (1) in table 2.1. Sources and order numbers: Wyeast 2308, White Labs WLP022, and Yeast Labs L33.

The Christian Schmidt strain has been the workhorse of small- and medium-sized breweries in the East and Midwest for decades. Ironically, only recently have complaints emerged about its instability. In the example involving the New York brewery, Christian Schmidt was rejected as their production yeast in favor of strain (2) in table 2.1 because of its instability. Sources and order numbers: Siebel BRY-118, Wyeast 2272, and BrewTech (unnumbered).

In our opinion, California Steam yeast is a stable version of Christian Schmidt, and both are closely related to the lager yeast culture originally brought to the United States (*One Hundred Years of Brewing* 1974). This strain has been conditioned to work well at relatively high temperatures for lagers (i.e., 60–62 °F [16–17 °C]), which is definitely not the case with W-34/70 or W-206. However, many brewers are switching to strains like this because the higher temperatures tend to reduce diacetyl faster and cut down on production time (Schmidt 1995). Sources and order numbers: BrewTech Cl-690, Wyeast 2112, White Labs WLP022, and Yeast Labs L35.

Ale Yeast

Saccharomyces cerevesia (the traditional name for top-fermenting ale yeast) has been used in baking and brewing for centuries; therefore, it is not surprising that genetic studies found considerable diversity in the chromosome fingerprints of these strains (Casey 1996). This diversity is also reflected in the functional classification of ale yeast, which is not nearly as tight as with lager strains. We grouped the yeast strains that share general characteristics.

Group 1—These are the so-called clean and neutral ale strains that tend to leave diacetyl and fusel alcohol levels well below threshold. Selected esters will be at or slightly above threshold, but this generally results in subtle, alelike flavor tones. The quality of beers made with these strains will by and large be determined by the quality of the recipe and the brewing materials used.

Version: Ballantine/Chico
- Optimal temperature: 68 °F (20 °C) (Note: This strain will ferment at much lower temperatures, however, ale characteristics tend to disappear at fermentation temperatures at or below 65 °F [18 °C].)
- Apparent attenuation: 75–76%
- Flocculation: Good
- Stability: Reasonable, so long as it is repitched in a timely manner after collection. It displays a strong tendency to mutate during liquid storage. Instabilities have also occurred when stored on slants by suppliers. The Ballantine/Chico strain has a long and proud history in North American ale brewing. Sources and order numbers: Siebel BRY-96, Wyeast 1056, BrewTech CL-10, White Labs WLP001, and Yeast Labs A02.

Version: German Kölsch
- Optimal temperature: 68 °F (20 °C)
- Apparent attenuation: 75–77%
- Flocculation: Medium
- Stability: Excellent

German Kölsch originates from the Bonn-Köln area where kölsch is brewed. This yeast tends to accent malt flavors to the point where some of the hop bitterness is blunted, and it strongly reduces ale fermentation products, including most, but not all, esters. The best of

An Analysis of Brewing Techniques

the German kölsch beer does have a definite hop character, and this is achieved by using a sufficiently high hop charge to bring the measured BU to the 28–30 milligrams per liter level. Beer pH, on the other hand, is typically in a range appropriate for ales (4.0–4.2), which is usually accompanied with a refreshing acidity. Sources and order numbers: Weihenstephan W-338, BrewTech CL450 (this strain is very close to W-338), Wyeast 1338 (this strain is also very close to W-338) and 2565 (this is a mixed ale/lager strain), White Labs WLP003.

Version: German Alt
- Optimal temperature: 62 °F (17 °C)
- Apparent attenuation: 76–78%
- Flocculation: Very strong
- Stability: Highly variable

German Alt strains tend to leave a dry and crisp finish. They are well suited to hoppy, alt-style beers. Sources and order numbers: BrewTech CL 400, Wyeast 1007, and Yeast Labs A06.

Version: Canadian ale
- Optimal temperature: 65 °F (18 °C)
- Apparent attenuation: 76–78%
- Flocculation: Medium/powdery
- Stability: Good

Canadian ale strains tend to mirror the characteristics of better Canadian ales in that beers produced with them typically have clean and pleasant flavors accompanied by well-defined fruity tones. These strains are also finding favor with selected microbreweries in both Canada and the United States. For example, Anchor's famous Liberty Ale is brewed with such a strain. Sources and order numbers: BrewTech CL-260, Wyeast 1272, and Yeast Labs A07.

Version: Scottish ale
- Optimal temperature: 55–60 °F (13–16 °C)
- Apparent attenuation: 69–72%
- Flocculation: Strong
- Stability: Good

Scottish ale strains are low-temperature, highly flocculant, alcohol-tolerant strains. Although they tend to have below average apparent attenuations, they ferment strong worts in the same way as dilute worts. As a consequence, these strains are well suited for a wide range of high-gravity ales. When fermented on the cold side, which is 55–60 °F (13–16 °C), they leave esters and fusel alcohol levels well below those obtained from other ale strains. Source and order number: Wyeast 1728.

Group 2—These yeast strains are the middle ground between the clean ale strains in group 1 and the idiosyncratic strains in group 3. Esters and/or diacetyl levels are typically slightly above threshold. However, if the yeast is in good condition, these flavors will rarely be regarded as defective. These strains have found wide acceptance among British ale brewers.

Version: London ale
- Optimal temperature: 68 °F (20 °C)
- Apparent attentuation: 75–77%
- Flocculation: Very strong
- Stability: Excellent

London ale strains have a characteristic full and rich flavor signature that accents maltiness. Ester levels are typically slightly above threshold, with diacetyl levels being at or slightly below threshold. Sources and order numbers: BrewTech CL-160, Wyeast 1968 and 1318, White Labs WLP002, and Siebel BRY-405.

Version: Burton ale
- Optimal temperature: 68 °F (20 °C)
- Apparent attenuation: 73–77%
- Flocculation: Medium
- Stability: Excellent

Burton yeast strains produce complex ales that tend to display citric and mineral tones, and a slightly woodlike flavor is sometimes detectable. These characteristics are seen in Worthington's White Shield, a classic Burton ale. If this yeast is roused during fermentation (i.e., Burton Union fermentation systems), diacetyl levels are likely to be high. Sources and order numbers: BrewTech CL-120, Wyeast 1028, and Yeast Labs A03.

Version: Whitbread
- Optimal temperature: 68 °F (20 °C)
- Apparent attenuation: 73-75%
- Flocculation: Medium
- Stability: In recent years, some versions have mysteriously lost their ability to metabolize trisaccharides, like maltotriose. This leads to an abnormally fast fermentation that comes to an abrupt halt once the apparent attenuation approaches 60-65%.

The original version of a Whitbread strain was a three-strain culture that had a characteristic dry, crisp, and slightly tart flavor profile (Fix, *Zymurgy* 1989). Sources and order numbers: Wyeast 1098 and Yeast Labs A04

Version: Guinness
- Optimal temperature: 68 °F (20 °C)
- Apparent attentuation: 71-75%
- Flocculation: Medium
- Stability: Good

Guinness yeast strains tend to give soft and full flavors. They tend to be very poor reducers of diacetyl, a problem compounded by the presence of gram-positive bacteria often seen in versions cultured from bottles. Not surprisingly, many feel these strains should be used only for porters and stouts. Sources and order numbers: BrewTech CL-240, Wyeast 1084, White Labs WLP004, and Yeast Labs A05.

Version: Norwich NCYC 1187
- Optimal temperature: 68 °F (20 °C)
- Apparent attenuation: 73-75%
- Flocculation: Strong
- Stability: Good

The Norwich NCYC 1187 yeast strain is the one that made the U.S. brewpub "seven-day wonder" possible. It is a very fast fermenter and is capable of being used on a seven-day cycle. Sources and order numbers: Food Research Institute NCYC 1187 and Wyeast (unnumbered).

Version: Ringwood
- Optimal temperature: 68 °F (20 °C)

- Apparent attentuation: 73–75%
- Flocculation: Good
- Stability: Good

Ringwood strains are the most complex of the group 2 strains. They tend to leave tangy, tart, fruitlike flavoring that sometimes has peppery/spicy undertones. This strain is very close to NCYC 1187 in most aspects. Sources and order numbers: BrewTech (unnumbered) and Yeast Labs A09.

Version: Australian/Cooper
- Optimal temperature: 68 °F (20 °C)
- Apparent attenuation: 75–77%
- Flocculation: Medium
- Stability: Good

Australian/Cooper yeast strains tend to promote a full flavor profile that has bready and sometimes nutty tones. Sources and order numbers: BrewTech CL-270, White Labs WLP006, and Yeast Labs A01.

Group 3—These are highly idiosyncratic yeast strains generally used only for special purposes.

Version: W-68
It was once felt that most Bavarian wheat beers were produced from a single strain, namely Weihenstephan W-68 (Warner 1992). Casey's studies, on the other hand, suggest there is actually considerable diversity among the strains being used commercially (Casey 1996). However, W-68 does have a number of favorable characteristics. This yeast leaves a soft clovelike flavor, and if the fermentation takes place at 71–72 °F (21–22 °C), there will also be banana undertones. Both flavors are traditional. Brewers should beware of different strains promoted as weizen yeast, as many are capable of producing highly unpleasant phenolic compounds. Sources and order numbers: Weihenstephan W-68; White Labs WLP008 and WLP009, and Wyeast 3068.

Version: Austin wheat
Austin wheat beer yeast has an impressive record with Belgian-style wheat beers. It leaves a soft and gentle phenolic flavor with a

very slight diacetyl undertone. This strain is finding acceptance with many brewpubs in the United States that produce upscale wheat beers. Brewers should be aware that this is not a user-friendly yeast strain and it often misbehaves. Sources and order numbers: BrewTech CL 980, White Labs WLP010 and WLP011, and Wyeast 3942 and 3944.

Version: Belgian lambic

Authentic Belgian lambic beers are fermented with a complex mix of microbes. (Guinard [1990]) provides an excellent survey of the yeast strains and bacteria that are relevant.) Such mixtures tend to impart a rich, earthy, acidic, and odiferous character to beer. Source and order number: Wyeast 3273.

Version: Belgian ale

As noted by Lodahl (1994), Belgian ale strains tend to be prolific ester and phenol producers, especially when the fermentation temperature is increased. Belgian ale yeasts are usually alcohol tolerant, flocculant, and highly attenuative. Originally, we hoped to give a detailed characterization of these strains; however, results from test brews were so contradictory that we decided against it. For example, none of the Duvel strains produced anything like the seductively clean and soft texture of the real Duvel. Yet in each case, the strain did a highly respectable job with a different Belgian style. Authenticity is not at issue here. Apparently, these strains behave differently in different brewing environments. In any case, we recommend that brewers be flexible and prepared to try different things; point of origin may be a poor guide of what to expect. Sources and order numbers: BrewTech CL300, CL320, CL328, and CL340; Wyeast 1214, 1388, 1762, and 3787; Siebel BRY-204; White Labs WLP012 and WLP013; and Yeast Labs A08.

STORAGE

Brewing yeast can be stored in a number of different ways. Table 2.2 lists the major options. The primary concern during yeast storage is the possibility of adverse changes taking place in the culture. Mutation is certainly a concern. This ranges from minor mutation, where flocculation and attenuation characteristics are slightly altered, to major mutation, where the culture undergoes a significant change in fermentative performance. Adverse environments (e.g., high temperature and/or extended storage) can create these effects. Starvation (lack of nutrients) can have similar effects. Another concern is the growth of beer-spoiling microorganisms during storage. Dormant yeasts sometimes experience a phenomenon called shock excretion, which is when selected amino acids are excreted from inside the cell membrane to the surrounding media (Fix, *Principles of Brewing Science* 1989). Various bacteria, especially gram-positive rods and cocci, use the excreted amino acids as both carbon and nitrogen sources for growth. In adverse circumstances, a trivial level of a foreign microbe can grow to completely unacceptable levels.

Table 2.2 Yeast Storage Methods

Form	Temperature	Safe Duration
Frozen cultures	*(-40--80 °C)	12 months
Slant (cultures in test tubes/petri dishes)	32–39 °F (0–4 °C)	4 months
Liquid with nutrients (packaged)	32–34 °F (0–1 °C)	1 week
Liquid with water or beer cover	32–34 °F (0–1 °C)	72 hours
Liquid with wort cover	32–34 °F (0–1 °C)	2 weeks

*See Raines (1995) for additional information.

The safest way to store yeast is to freeze it. Consequently, frozen storage is widely accepted among research laboratories. If major mutations and/or infections do occur, they are the result of processing errors (e.g., unclean conditions), not the storage method. We found, however, that minor mutations can occur in prolonged storage. A good working rule, though somewhat conservative, is to reculture frozen samples every twelve months. (See Raines [1992] for a detailed discussion of freezing yeast.)

Storing yeast cultures in test tubes or in petri dishes on a solidified wort-agar medium has been used by brewers throughout the twentieth century. This method, also known as the slant method, is just as safe as freezing. The only major difference between the two is that yeast stored on slants has to be recultured more frequently than frozen yeast. We found that reculturing slants every four months is a good rule. In any case, use caution when propagating yeast that has been stored on slants for more than six months. One reason slants have been so popular is that virtually all of important yeast strains can be purchased in this form from both large and small suppliers.

(The use and preparation of yeast slants are discussed in the Pitching Rates and Propagation sections later in this chapter.)

The riskiest way to store yeast is in liquid form. Interestingly, anecdotal evidence concerning the stability of liquid cultures varies significantly. Some brewers report satisfactory results with liquid yeast stored for six months or longer, while others report problems after only ten to twelve days.

Many brewers purchase yeast that is packaged with selected nutrients. In commercial breweries, where consistency and predictability are valued, this practice is widely used. A consulting laboratory does the initial propagation, after which the yeast is packaged with nutrients and sent by express mail to the brewery. It is then pitched within twenty-four to forty-eight hours. We found that the liquid yeast and nutrient mixture will be stable for at least a week if stored near 32 °F (0 °C), but after that, all bets are off.

Brewers who reuse their yeast must store it in liquid form. Storage under a sterile water cover is a common method and has an added benefit of helping remove trub and hop constituents from yeast. When the storage temperature is near 32 °F (0 °C), yeast can be kept for up to seventy-two hours without problem. However, a serious disadvantage of this method is associated with osmotic shock (Fix, *Principles of Brewing Science* 1989). This occurs when yeast is transferred from fermented beer to water, and the osmotic pressure on the cell walls undergoes a significant change. This can result in minor mutations. An alternative, albeit a more expensive one, is to store yeast under a sterile beer cover at 32 °F (0 °C). It is important that the beer be pasteurized; holding it at 176 °F (80 °C) for thirty minutes is sufficient.

Sometimes brewers need to keep collected yeast for more than seventy-two hours before it can be repitched. In such cases, a wort cover is needed. If the yeast is combined with an equal volume of wort and held near 32 °F (0 °C), it can be stored up to two weeks. It is important that the SG of the mixture be maintained at 1.020–1.040 by adding additional wort as required. We also want to emphasize that the acceptable margin for error with respect to infections in this procedure is virtually zero. Not only should the equipment be sterile, the wort should be pasteurized before each addition as well.

The number of times that yeast can be collected and repitched in new brews depends on several factors. The most important are:

- Level of sanitation in the brewery
- Stability of yeast strain with respect to mutation
- Ability of the brewery to meet the time limits of yeast storage

In ideal circumstances, yeast can be repitched indefinitely, and we know of breweries that have been repitching for years with excellent results. In less desirable environments, there are definite limits to the number of yeast generations. (The tests discussed later in the chapter can be used to determine whether a particular yeast slurry can be reused or if it needs to be discarded.)

PITCHING RATES

There have been a number of studies on the effects of yeast pitching rates on beer quality (Ibid.). The main points that emerged from this research are: (1) it is extremely important that a sufficient amount of yeast be pitched; and (2) in general, it is better to slightly overpitch than to underpitch. Underpitching can result in long lag times, elevated fermentation by-products, and elevated terminal gravities. These are damaging in that higher than normal terminal gravities skew the balance and flavor of a finished beer, and residual unfermented sugars are excellent carbon sources for bacteria.

The downside of overpitching is less damaging. Very high cell concentrations in wort typically lead to reduced yeast growth. This means that the yeast pitched will be the yeast cells responsible for the fermentation, which is a disadvantage only if the viability of the pitching yeast is below 90%. In the latter case, yeast/sulfury flavors can arise, possibly requiring longer than normal maturation times for the flavors to "age out." Also, beers that have been produced with elevated pitching rates may be harder to filter.

Research shows that a good rule for pitching cold-fermenting lager yeast is at a rate of 1.5×10^6 cells per milliliter for each 1 °P of wort. We found that pitching rates in the range 1-2 million cells per milliliter per °P of wort avoids the negative effects associated with overpitching or underpitching. These rates should be reduced by a factor of two for ale yeast fermented at ambient temperatures. For example, a 12 °P wort requires $1.5 \times 12 \times 10^6 = 18 \times 10^6$ cells per milliliter (plus or minus 6×10^6 cells per milliliter) for lager yeast and half that value for ale strains. (Accurate ways of counting yeast cells are discussed later in the chapter.)

There are many situations where a volumetric determination of a cell count is satisfactory. In this regard, it can be assumed that 1 milliliter yeast solids = 4.5×10^9 yeast cells. This means that 1 liter of yeast solids = 45×10^6 cells per milliliter when pitched into 1 hectoliter of wort. To return to the example of a 12 °P wort, our pitching rule requires $(12 \times 1.5) \div 45 = 0.4$ liters of yeast solids per hectoliter of wort for lager yeast. This is close to the rule of 0.5 liter yeast per hectoliter, often cited in the literature (Fix 1991). It is also close to the traditional rule (based on weight) of a pound of yeast per barrel (Vogel et al. 1946).

Uncertainty in the accuracy of volumetric determination of yeast cell counts is related to the uncertainty of the volume fraction of a slurry resulting from yeast solids. Figure 2.1 shows a yeast slurry after cooling and flocculation. Yeast solids are in the creamy middle layer of the sediment and represent 25% of the total volume. In lieu of additional information, we found 25% to be a good working approximation. In the example cited previously where 0.4 liter yeast solids per hectoliter were needed, the slurry size should be $0.4 \div 0.25 = 2$ liters per hectoliter for lager yeast and half that amount for ale strains.

Figure 2.1. Yeast slurry after cooling and flocculation.

PROPAGATION

Propagation is a process whereby a small amount of yeast inoculated from a slant is built up until there is enough yeast to pitch a full brew. (Brewers who purchase yeast in liquid form need only be concerned with the second stage of the propagation.) There are three stages of yeast propagation:

(1) The initial stage is the laboratory phase of propagation where a small number of cells are built up to a slurry of 2,000–2,400 milliliters in volume.
(2) The second stage takes place in the brewery where the slurry is built up to a point where there are slightly more yeast cells than needed for pitching.
(3) The final stage is the analytical part of the propagation where microscopy and staining techniques are used to determine the precise amount of yeast to be pitched.

The three most important aspects of yeast propagation are cell growth, selectivity, and climatization. Clearly, growth of yeast cells from the small number in the initial stages to an amount appropriate for pitching is key. However, growth is not an end in itself, and procedures sometimes used to speed growth, such as high temperatures or with media unnatural to beer, may not give the best results. What is needed is a timely buildup of yeast capable of making good beer. In the initial stage, this is done by inoculating a number of different samples and then selecting the best performers from them. As propagation proceeds, the yeast must be climatized by propagating them in a medium as close as possible in composition to the product wort into which they will ultimately be pitched.

Initial Stage of Propagation

Equipment and Materials—The following are required for the initial stage.

Transfer box: Propagation of microbes in modern research laboratories is done under highly sanitary conditions in specially cleaned rooms. Such an environment is difficult and often quite expensive to attain in an operating brewery. Using a transfer box, such as shown in figure 2.2, is an inexpensive and highly satisfactory alternative. Before use, the inside of the transfer box should be cleaned and sanitized

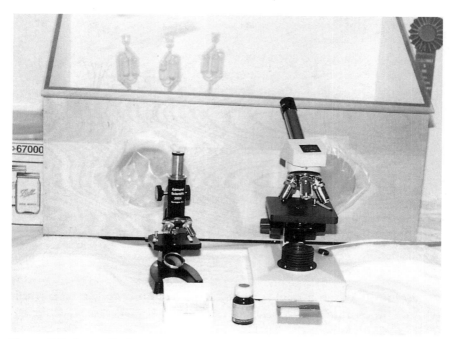

Figure 2.2. A transfer box.

with a Lysol™ solution or its equivalent. Once the box is sealed for yeast work, we recommend spraying the inside with a 70% alcohol solution before propagation.

Glassware: Eight 100-milliliter flasks, two 2,000-milliliter flasks, and a spare flask for rinse water (figure 2.3). These must be completely sterilized before use, preferably in an autoclave or a pressure cooker. If neither of these is available, immerse the flasks in boiling water for thirty minutes.

Inoculation loops: Ideally, eight stainless steel loops (see figure 2.4).

Miscellaneous: A propane blowtorch, a solution of 70% ethanol, and sterile cotton balls or parafilm to stopper propagation flasks.

Procedure—The initial stage is an eleven-step process, which includes initial wort propagation (2), pasteurization (3), initial selection (8), second wort change (9), second selection (10), and third wort change (11).

(1) Prepare transfer box and glassware. In addition, sterilize rinse water by boiling for fifteen minutes, and then add it to the spare flask.

Figure 2.3. Eight 100-millilter flasks, two 2,000-milliliter flasks, and one spare flask.

(2) Add 100 grams of dried malt extract to 750 milliliters of water and heat. When it begins to boil, add 1 gram of hop pellets. Boil for fifteen minutes. Measure SG and, if necessary, add water to reduce it to the 1.035–1.045 range.

(3) Strain 50 milliliters of the wort into each of the eight 100-milliliter flasks and stopper each with a cotton ball or parafilm. Pasteurize by holding the flasks at 176 °F (80 °C) for thirty minutes. Following this, cool them to the propagation temperature. We recommend 68 °F (20 °C) for ale yeast, and 59 °F (15 °C) for lager yeast.

(4) Flame each of the eight inoculation loops with the blowtorch, then immediately put them in the ethanol solution.

(5) Put all inoculation materials (wort, slants, loops, and rinse water) in the transfer box. Seal and spray the inside with the ethanol solution.

(6) Using the gloves on the transfer box, remove a loop from the ethanol solution and add it to the sterile rinse water. Open a slant and use the loop to transfer a small amount of yeast to the 100-milliliter flask. Replug the flask with the cotton ball or parafilm. Continue until all flasks are inoculated.

(7) Hold the flasks at the propagation temperature (cited in (3)), if necessary, using a water bath. Aerate by rousing on a regular basis. (Note: Approximately three to four slants are needed to inoculate eight propagation slants. If three or four slants are not available, we recommend first inoculating some petri dishes containing a solidified wort/agar media [see Slant Preparation and

An Analysis of Brewing Techniques

Figure 2.4. Inoculation loops.

Figure 2.5. A propane torch.

Inoculation for preparation instructions], then inoculating the propagation flasks with selected yeast from the petri dishes.)

(8) Small white dots appearing on the surface are the first signs of metabolic activity. This soon gives way to a full ferment, which is indicated by a full kraeusen appearing on the surface. The speed at which this occurs in the propagation flasks is a good measure of yeast viability and vigor. In this regard, the contents of any flask not active within forty-eight hours should be discarded. Usually, not more than one or two flasks need to be cast aside assuming the yeast inoculated from the slants was in good condition. Split the remaining flasks into two nearly equal groups (a and b), with group a consisting of the most vigorous yeast, group b the remaining ones that satisfy the forty-eight-hour criteria.

(9) Prepare and pasteurize wort that is equal to the volume of starters in groups a and b. Use the procedures described in (2) and (3), but pasteurize in the 2,000-milliliter flasks. Then cool the flasks to 68 °F (20 °C) if working with ale yeast, or to 57 °F (14 °C) with lager yeast. Add group a yeast to one flask and group b yeast to the other flask. Then seal the flasks with cotton balls or parafilm.

(10) Aerate the flasks by vigorous rousing on a regular basis until yeast activity is evident. The flask containing group a yeast should display metabolic activity almost immediately. In any case, the contents of any flask that are not active within twenty-four hours should be discarded. Allow the fermentation in the remaining flask to go to completion.

(11) Double the volume a second time with pasteurized wort and allow the fermentation to go to completion at 68 °F (20 °C) for ale yeast or 54 °F (12 °C) for lager yeast. At the end of the fermentation, cool the samples to 32 °F (0 °C).

Second Stage of Propagation

This is the brewery stage of propagation where the goal is to build the starter solution in 2,000-milliliter flasks into an amount slightly in excess of what is needed for pitching. In this stage, it is sufficient to use a volumetric determination of yeast cell numbers (see Pitching Rates section). A dedicated yeast propagator with a conical bottom, as shown in figure 2.6, is of great value. Ideally, the wort used should be as close as possible to the production wort, and the production fermentation temperatures should be used. A geometric increase in wort volume works well during the brewery stage of propagation, increasing volumes by factors of two (i.e., four, eight, sixteen, etc.) at each step until the estimated target volume is achieved. It is also useful to let the yeast go beyond the high kraeusen stage of fermentation before adding new wort. In addition, in the final step leading to the target volume, let the yeast go through a full fermentation cycle before cooling to 32 °F (0 °C) at the end.

When brewers are strapped for time, many directly pitch the lab slurry into a mini brew. When the mini-brew is at high kraeusen, a sufficient amount of wort is added to bring it to a full brew size. Beer produced from such "first-generation yeast" often has off-flavors and has to be blended or discarded. Underpitching is often the culprit in such circumstances.

Final Stage of Propagation

At this stage, we are in the same position as if the yeast had been collected from a previous brew. The objective here is to repitch the right amount of good yeast. After cooling, a yeast layer forms that has three distinct layers:

(1) The good yeasts are in the middle layer, characterized by its light color and a thick, creamy consistency. Yeasts from this layer have a clean taste and smell.

(2) The bottom layer typically consists of trub and bitter-tasting hop materials.

(3) The top layer consists of more debris, and if bacteria are present, they typically will be in this layer.

Virtually all of the middle yeast layer can be collected with a conical-bottomed propagator without contamination from the top and bottom layers.

Having collected the yeast to be pitched, the tests described in the Evaluation of Yeast section should be done.

Figure 2.6. Yeast propagator.

OXYGENATION OF CHILLED WORT

It is crucial that a sufficient amount of oxygen be dissolved in wort at the start of fermentation, because yeast uses the oxygen in aerobic respiration to build up the metabolic energy needed to fuel the energy-consuming anaerobic fermentation. Deficiencies in the oxygen content in chilled wort result in problems similar to those associated with underpitched yeast, including undesirable lags in the start of fermentation, elevated fermentation products (especially esters), and high final gravities.

The exact oxygen demand of yeast depends on a number of factors. First, while there are vast differences in strains, in general, yeasts that have extremely high oxygen demands have not found acceptance in brewing. Certainly, none of the strains in the major categories cited in the Strains section (groups 1 and 2, lager and ale yeast) has displayed abnormalties with respect to oxygen demand.

The physiological condition of yeast is also extremely important. Yeasts that test out at 95% viability typically need only 4–5 milligrams per liter of oxygen when pitched into worts of normal gravity (i.e.,

Yeast

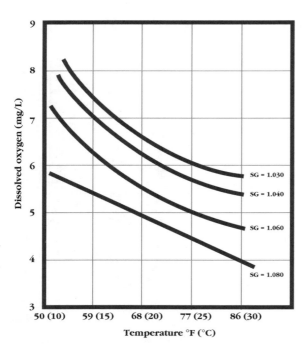

Figure 2.7. Maximum dissolved oxygen in wort versus temperature at various SGs.

12 °P or below). As wort gravity increases, so does yeast oxygen demand. For example, 95% viable yeast (or better) pitched into 15 °P wort generally needs 8-10 milligrams of oxygen. Moreover, the oxygen demand increases sharply as the wort gravity exceeds 15 °P.

The 95% or better viability is very important. For example, yeast in the 80-90% viability range requires at least 8-10 milligrams per liter of oxygen in even worts of 12 °P or lower. Moreover, once yeast viability falls below 80%, it may be impossible to compensate the deficiency with oxygen.

Wort oxygen concentrations are displayed in figure 2.7 at various temperatures and SGs. Data were generated with the following procedure:

(1) The Zahm and Nagel tank, shown in figure 2.8, was used as an oxygenator.
(2) A 0.5 micron diffusing stone was attached to the gas line of the tank in figure 2.8.
(3) After wort was transferred into the tank, oxygen was added via the gas line.
(4) A spray of small oxygen bubbles from the diffusing stone assisted in dissolving the oxygen into wort.

An Analysis of Brewing Techniques

The regulator on the oxygen tank was set at 20 pounds per square inch (psi), and the cock on the tank's cap was partially open to allow a slight gas bleed. (See also the feed and bleed carbonation procedure described in the Carbonation section of chapter 5.) In each feeding session, oxygen was injected until foam began to appear at the outlet valve on the tank's cap. At that point, all cocks were closed until the next feeding session. The following two schedules were used:

Strong wort oxygenation: Seven oxygen feeds were done during a thirty-minute interval. This gave the highest final dissolved oxygen level we were able to achieve with our system (figure 2.7).

Figure 2.8. A Zahm and Nagel tank.

Weak wort oxygenation: Three feeds were done during a ten-minute interval. Final dissolved oxygen values were less consistent than those obtained from the strong wort oxygenation procedure, however, they did fall between 67% and 75% of the values shown in figure 2.7.

After the oxygen feeding, the oxygenated wort was pumped into a unitank, shown in figure 2.9. The fill, from the bottom of the tank, was done under ambient pressure. When the tank was filled, a sample was removed from the cock at the top of the cone, and the oxygen reading was done with a dissolved oxygen meter from Fisher Scientific (Orion model 820).

The pressure gauge on the Zahm and Nagel tank indicated that very high oxygen levels were achieved in

Figure 2.9. A unitank.

the tank during oxygen feeds, values in excess of 20 milligrams per liter being common. The data in figure 2.7, on the other hand, demonstrate that the ambient fill of the fermenter led to significant depressurization. Similar effects are seen in commercial in-line wort oxygenation systems. (See Reuther and Brandon [1994] for a detailed experimental and theoretical analysis of a system typical of those currently being used in modern breweries.) Their in-line dissolved oxygen values approached 30 milligrams per liter, however, during the filling of the fermenter, they fell into a range similar to that given in figure 2.7.

Some experts have suggested that air rather than oxygen be used, since the latter can be toxic to yeast. This is a theoretical possibility, however, the idea confuses peak dissolved oxygen values with those values actually available to yeast. It is our view that if an ambient oxygenation system, such as previously described, is used, it is impossible to get near-lethal oxygen levels in practical brewing situations. A more legitimate concern regarding oxygen injection is the converse, namely, that high oxygen levels can be too stimulatory, causing higher than normal cell growth rates, which result in elevated ester levels. We have not seen this effect in ambient systems, but it is a valid concern with the systems we will discuss below.

Selected data in the literature suggest that the maximum oxygen values achieved with our system may be slightly lower than theoretical saturation levels. For example, de Clerck (1957) reported that a 14 °P wort at normal temperature has an oxygen saturation level of 6.5 milligrams per liter, while a 7 °P wort has 7.9 milligrams per liter. Using 63.5 °F (17.5 °C) as "normal temperature," our maximum readings from figure 2.7 are 6.0 and 7.1 milligrams per liter, respectively. However, these differences are not great enough to change the qualitative conclusions we have drawn.

We also did selected batches using compressed air in place of oxygen. Compressed air is attractive to commercial brewers since it is considerably cheaper than oxygen. Atmospheric air is approximately 78% nitrogen, 21% oxygen, and 1% argon. Nitrogen is not particularly soluble in beer, and as a consequence, the oxygen fraction of air dissolved in beer is around 32%. In the Zahm and Nagel system previously discussed, we were able to get dissolved oxygen readings close to those cited in figure 2.7, however considerably more effort was required. The required number of feeds increased sharply (sometimes by a factor of ten or more). In addition, there was considerable variation in the final fermenter dissolved oxygen readings with even small changes in the injection schedules. On the other hand, well-engineered commercial in-line systems have been designed in such a way that these difficulties are avoided.

The major defect of ambient oxygenation systems is that they are not adequate for high-gravity brews. Barley wines are a striking example. There are three factors at work here and all are negative: (1) there is suppression of oxygen absorption due to temperature (68 °F [20 °C] versus the 41–50 °F [5–10 °C] used for lagers); (2) there is suppression due to elevated wort gravity; (3) there is increased yeast oxygen demand, also due to elevated wort gravity. Perhaps this is the basis for the old British saying that the best way to evaluate ale strains is to see what kind of job they do with barley wines. While it is true that yeast selection is very important for high-gravity beers, additional improvements can be made if further steps are taken to deal with oxygen deficiency. The following have been proposed:

(1) Trub carry-over: Lipids from trub can be used in part as oxygen substitutes. In addition, trub particles serve as nucleation sites for carbon dioxide evolution. This has the benefit of reducing carbon dioxide suppression of yeast metabolism. On the other hand, lipids from trub that are not utilized by yeast spill over into the finished beer where they can be big players in beer staling. As a consequence, the literature is unclear regarding the practical value of using turbid worts to compensate for wort oxygen deficiencies (see Fix, *Principles of Brewing Science* 1989). It is our opinion that the benefits of reasonably clear worts prevail and that oxygen deficiency be dealt with in other ways.

(2) Yeast aeration/oxygenation: Yeast slurry to be pitched can be combined with some wort into which air or oxygen is injected. This method has proven to be quite effective in commercial brewing (Schmidt 1995).

   We tested two versions of yeast aeration—weak yeast oxygenation and strong yeast aeration. In the procedure, 5 liters of a wort/yeast solution were added to a 19-liter keg. The lid of the keg was not attached, and oxygen was injected through the liquid line of the keg. Within ten to fifteen seconds, the keg filled with foam. The contents were then poured into the fermenter, followed by the addition of wort, oxygenated by standard ambient procedures. In the strong yeast aeration procedure, yeast and wort were aerated together in the fermenter. (Sterile air is used for this in commercial practice, and the feed is maintained so that a dissolved oxygen value of 8–10 milligrams per liter is obtained. Since this is done under pressure, much higher dissolved oxygen values than those reported in figure 2.7 can be achieved.)

Our test brews indicate that weak yeast oxygen is a good general procedure that improves performance in all circumstances. It is particularly helpful when wort gravities fall in the 12–16 °P range. However, it is not completely effective with a wort gravity of 18 °P or higher, in which case some version of strong yeast aeration is needed. Care should be taken to monitor the dissolved oxygen levels achieved, since negative effects have been seen in practical brewing situations using this type of closed system. For example, Donhauser and Wagner (1996) conducted a sensory analysis of beers aerated and/or oxygenated with a number of different systems. The lowest marks went to a beer oxygenated in a closed system; in fact, the beer rated below one where neither aeration nor oxygenation had been used. Although reasons for this are not cited, it is likely that the negative sensory response was due to the yeast overstimulation effect previously discussed. This study was confined to lager beer, therefore, it did not address how these issues would play out in barley wines. Additional research is needed in this area.

(3) Aeration during fermentation: This procedure was first proposed by Raines (Raines, personal communication). The idea is to inject sterile air into the fermenter during the aerobic part of fermentation. (A variation of this method was investigated and found to be favorable [Schmidt 1995].) The widely used commercial practice of incrementally filling fermenters is closely related to this procedure. Timing is crucial, and it is important that aeration be started promptly and terminated in a timely manner in order to prevent repression of anaerobic fermentation via the Pasteur effect. For example, Donhauser and Wagner (1996) reported that negative effects were found when aeration was started twenty-four hours after pitching.

(4) High pitching rates: It has been our experience that small-scale brewers normally underpitch yeast, and any recommendation that calls for increased yeast is usually accompanied by improvements in the finished beer. However, recent recommendations go beyond this in that high pitching rates (above those cited in

the Pitching Rate section) are proposed as an alternative to wort aeration/oxygenation. Theoretically, this is possible, since oxygen is used primarily to stimulate yeast growth and overpitching presumably makes such growth unnecessary. Abnormally high pitching rates have been studied and rejected in the context of commercial brewing. The primary reason is that beers made this way are extremely hard to filter and display poor stability with respect to clarity once packaged. The relevance of these results for unfiltered beer remains an open question, and additional study in practical brewing situations needs to be done. Until these issues are clarified, we remain somewhat skeptical that abnormally high pitching rates are a viable option.

(5) Large yeast starters: This procedure is attractive in part because yeast performance is maximized by repitching in a timely manner after collection. If one is willing to collect yeast from the starter using standard procedures (see Pitching Rates section) and to discard the starter after this is done, then there is much to say for this method. However, adding the entire contents of a starter is likely to add undesirable constituents (particularly oxidized products) which can spill over to the finished product.

Table 2.3 summarizes the material discussed in this section.

Table 2.3 Wort Oxygenation
(90% yeast viability or better is assumed)

Wort Original Extract (°P)	Minimum O$_2$ Level (mg/L)	Lager Procedure	Ale Procedure
10–12	5–6	WWO	WWO
12–14	6–8	WWO, WYO	SWO, WYO
14–16	8–10	SWO, WYO	SWO, SYA
16–18	10–12	SWO, SYA	SWO, SYA, use of an alcohol-tolerant yeast strain

Note: "Ale" refers to a beer fermented and oxygenated at approximately 68 °F (20 °C), and "lager" refers to one where the temperature is near 50 °F (10 °C). WWO = weak wort oxygenation; SWO = strong wort oxygenation; SYA = strong yeast aeration; WYO = weak yeast oxygenation.

SLANT PREPARATION AND INOCULATION
There are two steps involved in the preparation of new slants. The first involves adding the proper media to test tubes or petri dishes.

Once prepared, the slants store well for a long time when refrigerated, so many can be prepared at one time. The second step consists of inoculating the slants with yeast (this is the exact reverse of the propagation procedure described in the Propagation section).

Media Preparation

Equipment and Materials—The following are needed to make slants in test tubes:

(1) Test tubes: These should be 20 millimeters x 150 millimeters and have screw caps.
(2) Media: This typically consists of malt extract and agar. (Some suppliers sell prepared mixtures, such as the Bacto Universal Beer Agar Medium, marketed by Wyeast Laboratories, which is widely used.)
(3) Autoclave or pressure cooker.

Procedure—To prepare media, do the following:

(1) As a general rule, measure 4 tablespoons of malt extract and 1 tablespoon of agar per 1 cup of water to yield sixteen to eighteen slants.
(2) Bring the water to a boil, then stir in the malt extract. Boil for ten minutes.
(3) Remove from heat and then start stirring in the agar. This takes some effort, but good solidification is the reward. (Gelatin is easier to dissolve, but sometimes it does not give proper solidification.)
(4) When the agar is dissolved, add the malt/agar solution to the test tubes, filling each to approximately one-half of their volume. Add the screw cap, but do not fully tighten.
(5) Autoclave the tubes at 15 psi for five minutes.
(6) Tighten the caps on the tubes and place them at a thirty-degree angle. Allow them to solidify at room temperature. Solidification should become apparent within a few hours. If the mixture does not solidify after twenty-four hours, then the liquid should be discarded.
(7) Refrigerate until needed.

Since petri dishes cannot be autoclaved, alternate procedures are needed. A common practice is to autoclave the malt/agar solution in small jars and then pour it into the petri dishes. It is important that the latter is done in a transfer box, since superfluous infections are not uncommon. It is also a good idea to leave petri dishes prepared this way at 77–86 °F (25–30 °C) for one to two weeks to make sure bacteria and/or mold are not present. (Mold will be visible at the end of that time period.) While petri dishes take more work to prepare than test tubes, they do offer the advantage of having more surface area. After the trial period, the dishes should be sealed with electrician's tape and refrigerated.

As mentioned previously, inoculation of slants is essentially the reverse of the propagation procedure described in the Propagation section. Instead of removing yeast from slants and inoculating them in flasks, yeast in flasks are added to slants. Therefore, the same equipment is needed for the laboratory phase of propagation as was listed in the Propagation section.

Inoculating the Slants

(1) Prepare transfer box, test tubes, and a flask for yeast collection (see the Yeast Propagation section).

(2) Carefully collect a sample of yeast in the flask, then seal it with parafilm. Inoculation should be done immediately after collection.

(3) Flame inoculation loops with a blowtorch and put them in the alcohol solution.

(4) Put all materials inside the transfer box, seal, and spray the inside with a 70% alcohol solution.

(5) First open a test tube. Remove a loop from the alcohol solution and place it in the yeast solution. Slowly insert the loop into the test tube, avoiding contact with either the sides or neck of the tube. Streak the yeast over the solid in a thin layer, covering as much of the surface area as possible. Slowly remove the loop, avoiding contact with the sides or neck. Place the screw cap back on the tube and tighten. When finished, store the tubes at 77 °F (25 °C) for one week. Visually inspect all the tubes during the week to check for both yeast growth and for any irregularities. Discard those that are not satisfactory. Store the remainder at 35–47 °F (2–8 °C). After three to four months of storage, unused tubes should either be discarded or recultured (i.e., propagated by the procedures in the Pitching Rates section and then put on fresh slants). It is best to put production yeast on slants on a regular basis so that reculturing is not necessary. The larger surface area afforded by petri dishes is useful in that yeast can be streaked in parallel lines that angle each other, thus allowing better

examination of growth patterns. Petri dishes should be sealed after the one-week trial period with electrician's tape and refrigerated.

EVALUATING PITCHING YEAST

In this section we discuss the tests that can be used to evaluate pitching yeast, and we provide step-by-step instructions. The first two procedures deal with microscopic cell counts (*ASBC Methods of Analysis,* 8th ed., 1992) and estimating cell viability.

Microscopic Cell Counts

Equipment and Materials—The following are needed to test microscopic cell counts:

(1) Microscope: A monocular (one eyepiece) scope capable of 200–400 magnification is adequate. High-quality student microscopes are available at reasonable prices and are more than adequate for these tests.
(2) Micropipette: A 1-milliliter fine tip and a 10-milliliter volumetric.
(3) Hemocytometer: A glass chamber (figure 2.10) with two counting grids (figure 2.11). Each grid has nine 1-mm^2 squares; the central square is where the actual counting is done (figure 2.12). The central square has twenty-five subsquares, which in turn are divided into sixteen smaller subsquares. The volume of the central square is 10^{-4} cm^3, so each of the twenty-five subsquares has a volume of $(1/25) \times 10^{-4} = 4 \times 10^{-6}$ cm^3. This is the same as 4×10^{-6} mL.

Figure 2.10. Hemocytometer.

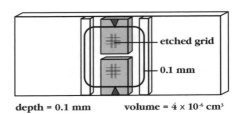

depth = 0.1 mm   volume = 4×10^{-6} cm^3

Figure 2.11. Diagram of hemocytometer showing two counting grids and correct positioning of the cover slide.

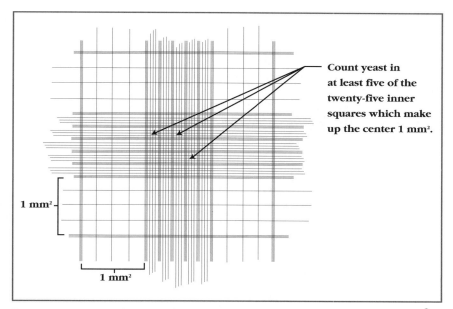

Count yeast in at least five of the twenty-five inner squares which make up the center 1 mm².

1 mm²

1 mm²

Figure 2.12. Magnification of etched grid. Area corresponding to 1 mm² is shown as well as etched pattern at low magnification (x 40).

Procedure—Following are the seven steps involved in microscopic cell counting:

(1) Make sure the counting grid and cover slide are clean and dry. Lens paper and a 70% alcohol solution are usually used.

(2) Place cover slip over counting area.

(3) Collect a sample to be evaluated from the yeast solids. Remove yeast clumps by mixing well. We find it useful to dilute 1 milliliter of the yeast solid with 9 milliliters of distilled water; the dilution factor used in the counting formula will then be ten, otherwise the factor is one. It is also beneficial to add a 0.5% acetic or sulfuric acid solution to retard yeast growth during counting (Raines 1995).

(4) Use the micropipette to apply a small drop of the sample onto the bottom counting chamber. Capillary action should suck the sample up underneath the cover slide.

(5) Carefully place the hemocytometer on the microscope stage. We like to define the field of view at a rather low magnification, say x 40 (x 10 eyepiece and x 4 objective). Following this, we frame up to x 400 (x 40 objective) to do the actual counts.

(6) Ideally, one should count the yeast in all twenty-five squares. However, if they appear to be uniform in density, counts can be done in the most representative squares. We usually like to do at least five of the twenty-five squares.

(7) Compute the cell concentrations with the following:

$$\text{concentration (cells/mL)} = \frac{(\text{dilution factor}) \times (\text{total number of cells counted}) \times 2.5 \times 10^5}{(\text{number of squares used})}$$

Suppose the following cells were counted:

1			5
	13		
21			25

The sample was diluted as in (3) (dilution factor of ten), and the counts are:

Square	Number of Cells
1	7
5	8
13	8
21	8
25	7
Total	**38**

The yeast cell concentration is then computed using the formula:

concentration = (10) (38) (2.5) (10^5) / (5) = 19 x 10^6 cells/mL.

We find it useful to load the top counting chamber and repeat (1) through (7). If the two yeast cell concentrations differ by more than 10–20%, serious consideration should be given to scrapping the results and starting over with new counts.

An Analysis of Brewing Techniques

Cell Viability via Staining

In most practical brewing situations, the negative effects that are usually associated with underpitching do not actually arise from too low a cell count, but rather from the low level of viability of the cells pitched. A 95% viability criterion is a worthy if somewhat conservative objective, however, it has been our experience that slurries with less than 90% viability are not suitable for top-quality beer.

A number of dyes are used for yeast staining, including methylene blue, rhodamine B, and acridine orange. Viable cells contain sufficient amounts of nicotinamido adenine dinucleotide (NADH) (Fix, *Principles of Brewing Science* 1989) to metabolize dye and do not change color when dye is added. Dead and weak cells will stain (i.e., undergo a color change).

Many brewers combine staining with cell counts, using the bottom chamber of the hemocytometer for counting and the top chamber for staining. If this is done, omit the acid charge in (3) of the cell counting procedure. It should be noted, however, that it is also possible to get reasonable viability results using only a glass slide and a cover slip rather than a hemocytometer.

Of the available dyes, we get the best results with rhodamine B when viabilities are in the 80–100% range, but when viability is below 70%, results tend to be erratic. However, we do not see this as a practical issue, since yeasts with viabilities below 90%, in our opinion, are unsuitable, regardless of whether the actual viability is 80%, 70%, or less.

Preparing Rhodamine B Dye—Prepare a 1% weight to volume solution of citric acid in distilled water. Adjust pH to 6.0 with sodium hydroxide. Use this buffer to make a 0.2% solution of rhodamine B. Add a few drops of phenol alcohol to inhibit bacterial growth. Filter this liquid to remove turbidity.

Procedure—To test for yeast viability, mix two drops of yeast sediment with one drop of rhodamine B. Add a cover slip and examine at x 200–400 with a microscope. Nonviable yeast cells stain red. A variety of bacteria stain pinkish red, but they are detectable only at high levels of infection at a magnification of 1,000 using an oil immersion microscope.

Iodine Test for Glycogen

Glycogen is a carbohydrate that serves as an important food reserve for yeast. Glycogen deficiency is usually contiguous with low cell viability, hence it can be determined by staining. It is also possible to

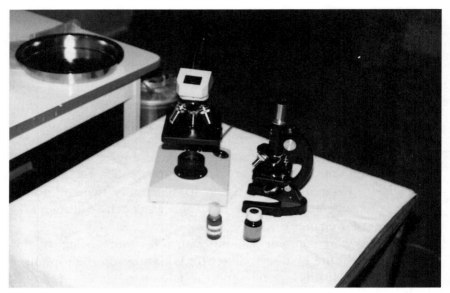

Figure 2.13. Yeast stains and microscopes.

attain a reasonable estimate of the glycogen level directly, using a simple iodine test that does not require the use of a microscope.

The scientific basis for the test is that glycogen, being a highly branched polysaccharide, reacts with iodine. In this regard, the test is similar to the iodine test for starch in mashing, except that in this case the color is slightly different and a strong, very dark brown reaction is good news. As the glycogen level decreases, the sample becomes progressively more yellow.

Procedure—Combine 1 milligram per milliliter iodine crystals and 10 milligrams per milliliter potassium iodine crystals in distilled water. (We usually work with 100-milliliter solutions that require 0.1 gram of iodine crystals and 1 gram of potassium iodine crystals.) Next, put 10 milliliters of yeast slurry on a clear white surface. Add one drop of the iodine solution. Wait for coloring to stabilize and observe its intensity.

This test has two limitations: (1) the iodine solution is not specific for glycogen and will react with other starchy material in the slurry if present; and (2) it is necessary to wait until the solution starts to enter the cell walls, since that is where glycogen is stored in yeast. This usually happens within a few minutes, and certainly not longer than an hour. An important feature of a vigorous yeast crop is

An Analysis of Brewing Techniques

the viability of its intercellular transport system. Thus, the time it takes the iodine solution to react is also of practical interest. Our own criterion is that a well-defined, dark brown color should be established within ten minutes.

Test for Gram-Positive Bacteria

It is impossible in any practical brewing situation to keep the pitching yeast totally free of harmful bacteria. However, if cell counts and cell viability meet the correct criteria (i.e., the cell counts cited in the Pitching Rates section and 95% viability), low bacterial levels will not be an issue in finished beer quality. (We consider low bacterial levels to be less than fifty cells per milliliter.) In addition, it is usually sufficient to check only for gram-positive rods (*Lactobacillus*) and cocci (*Pediococcus*).

An elementary, user-friendly medium that is capable of meeting objectives is Hsu's *Lactobacillus Pediococcus* media (HLP). However, it is also a crude medium, primarily because it uses sulfates (see table 2.4) to create anaerobic conditions. Sulfates are essential in order to detect *Lactobacillus* and *Pediococcus*, but because sulfuric acid is partially harmful to bacteria, the procedure will always undercount the number of bacteria present. Nevertheless, we found that the undercount is never more than a factor of ten in the case of rods and less than a factor of five in the case of cocci. Thus, if the HLP analysis indicates the presence of two rods per milliliter and three cocci per milliliter, this should be interpreted as not more than 2 x 10 = 20 rods per milliliter and not more than 3 x 5 = 15 cocci per milliliter.

Table 2.4 Chemical Makeup of HLP*

Component	Percent
Agar	2.00
Sodium acetate	4.00
Tomato juice broth	29.00
Malt extract	7.00
Peptone	7.00
Calcium pantothenate	1.00
Citric acid	2.00
Dextrin	0.10
Sodium sulfate	2.00
Sodium thioglycolate	1.00
Cycloheximide	0.01

*From J. E. Siebel Sons' Co., Inc., HLP Medium Safety Data Sheet.

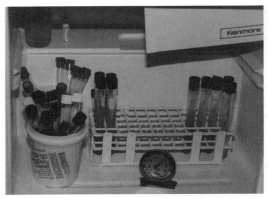

Figure 2.14. Hsu's *Lactobacillus Pediococcus* media (HLP) and HLP tubes.

Equipment and Materials—HLP, sixteen 150-millimeter test tubes, pipettes, water bath capable of maintaining 86 °F (30 °C), and syringe.

Preparing the Medium—Use 7 grams of HLP per 100 milliliters of water. (Distilled is preferred over tap.) Each test tube should contain 25 milliliters of dissolved medium, so 400 milliliters of water for

Figure 2.15. Tubes being heated.

An Analysis of Brewing Techniques

the sixteen tubes. The tubes will keep if refrigerated, so it is convenient to prepare many tubes at one time. Follow these steps:

(1) Sterilize test tubes and syringe.
(2) Bring water to a boil.
(3) Stir in HLP powder and hold at a boil for three minutes.
(4) Remove from heat and add 25 milliliters of medium to test tubes with the syringe.
(5) Store tubes in a refrigerator (see figure 2.14).

Inoculating the Yeast—Inoculation can be done in a transfer box, however, our experience has shown that this is not necessary. A clean working area will do, although we suggest scrubbing the work area with a Lysol™ solution, or an equivalent disinfectant, beforehand. The manufacturer of HLP suggests putting pipette 0.1–1 milliliter of sample into the tube. However, we believe that a full milliliter (1 milliliter) should be added, which is the maximum amount HLP can support. Specific steps are as follows:

(1) Sterilize pipettes.
(2) Heat tubes to be inoculated (two or three per 5 gallons is sufficient) to 176 °F (80 °C) (figure 2.15). Let them cool to 104 °F (40 °C), the temperature at which inoculation should take place.
(3) Pipette 1 milliliter of sample into each tube. Try to remove liquid from the top of the yeast layer, but maximize the amount of yeast added (see figure 2.16).
(4) Invert the tubes several times to dissolve the sample.
(5) Place tubes in a water bath at 86 °F (30 °C) for seventy-two hours (see figure 2.17).

Figure 2.16. Tubes with 1-milliliter sample.

Figure 2.17. Tubes in water bath.

Yeast

The presence of *Lactobacillus* is indicated by tornadolike strings in the bottom two-thirds of the tube. Each tornado structure represents one cell that grew in the tube. Since 1 milliliter of sample was added, the number of tornado structures gives the number of rods per milliliter. As noted previously, this is likely an undercount by, at most, a factor of ten. *Pediococcus* presents as oval structures that resemble rugby balls. Cocci are less sensitive to acids than rods, so this undercount is at most a factor of five.

Yeasts show up as a cloud throughout the tube. If there is too much yeast carry-over, the yeast cloud can obscure the visual identification of bacteria. The manufacturer suggests using membrane filtration, an alternative that solves the problem and also tends to give lower undercounts.

According to the manufacturer, a dense cloud at the top of the tube indicates the presence of aerobic bacteria relevant to beer; however, we found that this is not necessarily the case. Virtually anything can be at the top, including aerobics, yeast, and/or microbes not relevant to beer. This is, of course, a defect common to "artificial" media (i.e., media that is unlike beer), which is why HLP should only be used as a test for *Lactobacillus* and *Pediococcus* in pitching yeast.

Test for Gram-Negative Bacteria

It has been our experience that gram-negative bacteria, like *Escherichia coli*, assorted coliforms, and *Obesumbacterium*, gain entry into the fermenter primarily through wort. Selected gram positives also make their initial appearance this way. As a consequence, it is useful to determine the purity of the wort at pitching.

Procedure—Remove approximately 500 milliliters of chilled and aerated wort just before the yeast is pitched. Hold this sample in a water bath at 86 °F (30 °C) until instabilities become apparent. This includes the formation of haze, gas production, or any other hints of metabolic activity. (See table 2.5 for water bath guidelines.)

It is relatively easy to identify the type of microbes present. Traditionally, this procedure is called the "sniff and snort test," because once the sample becomes unstable, its aroma usually indicates the cause. Gram negatives are usually big sulfur producers, and their presence is indicated by a strong cornlike smell or those of rotten vegetables and/or parsnip. An acidic/bacterial smell usually means that thermophilic lactic acid bacteria (most likely *Lactobacillus delbrueckii*) are present.

If you have doubts about what microbes are present, use the following simple equivalent of a gram strain. Using a sterile loop, place part of the sediment on a sterile glass surface. With a separate sterile loop, add a 3% aqueous solution of potassium hydroxide. Gram-negative microbes become viscous when mixed with potassium hydroxide, while gram-positive bacteria do not react.

Table 2.5 Water Bath Guidelines

Length of Stable Period	Comments
< 24 hours	This represents a serious wort infection. Finished beer flavors will likely be affected.
24–48 hours	This is a less serious situation, although still unacceptable. Finished beer will be affected only in subtle ways.
48–72 hours	Finished beer will not be affected, although this condition is an indication that the system of sanitation being used is inadequate.
> 72 hours	The desirable situation.

Test for Mutants

Mutated yeast are best classified in terms of their functional disorders. The most common disorders are (1) loss of flocculation; (2) loss of ability to ferment sugars, like maltotriose; and (3) respiratory deficiencies. The first two are the easiest to detect at low levels, since defects tend to gradually increase through generations. Respiratory-deficient mutants are the most subtle and potentially the most dangerous. These mutants are capable of creating elevated diacetyl and fusel alcohol levels, and as a consequence, they are often confused with bacterial infections. Since respiratory-deficient mutants arise from abusive treatment (discussed in the Strains and Storage sections) and not unclean conditions, this misunderstanding can lead brewers in the wrong direction when they are looking for practical solutions. The following staining test can be used to identify respiratory-deficient mutants. It is similar in role and scope to the staining procedures for yeast viability.

Equipment and Materials—MYGP medium (Difco), triphenyl tetrazolium red, 0.06 M potassium phosphate buffer (pH = 7.0), filter membrane, petri dishes, forceps, microscope (x 200).

Procedure—Prepare a stock containing 0.1% triphenyl tetrazolium red in 0.06 M potassium phosphate buffer. (Stock can be stored in brown bottles in a freezer.) Start the test by growing yeast in a petri dish on a filter membrane with the MYGP medium until a colony 1–2 millimeters in diameter is achieved. Use the forceps to transfer the filter membrane to a new petri dish. Saturate with tetrazolium red stock solution. Within a few minutes, normal yeast cells will start staining red; this will continue for two to four hours. Respiratory-deficient mutants remain unstained.

It is our opinion that if the level of respitory-deficient mutants is below 1%, finished beer flavor will not be affected. Serious flavor disorders occur when respiratory-deficient mutants account for 10–20% (or more) of the total.

Tests for Wild Yeast

The majority of off-flavors in craft beer—amateur or commercial—are the result of using noncultured yeast. There are a large number of relevant strains, however, the most detrimental fall into one of three categories: superattenuators, *Brettanomyces*, or vino strains.

Superattenuators: *Saccharomyces diastaticus* is the most common example. These strains can metabolize virtually all of the wort sugars, including complex dextrins. In the process, they produce unmistakably nasty medicinal flavors. Fortunately, these yeasts are easy to detect, even at low levels, before they can influence beer.

Our favorite way to detect them is with a liter-sized pilot fermentation at 77 °F (25 °C), using wort produced from dextrin malt extracts. These usually have a RDF of around 10%, however, the actual RDF needs to be determined before you begin the test. When *S. diastaticus* is present at levels as low as 100 cells per milliliter, the actual RDF is much higher than what is found in a pure culture. In addition, each tenfold increase in the wild yeast concentration increases the RDF by a factor of approximately one and one-half to two. At a level of 100,000 cells per milliliter or higher, they will start to control the entire fermentation.

Brettanomyces: This genera and its sporulating equivalent, *Dekkera*, have been used to produce select Belgian and strong English ales. Accidental contamination, on the other hand, can have deleterious effects. These strains produce copious amounts of acetic acid and phenolic compounds. Thus, ciderlike tones and clove/medicinal aromas will be noted. They also produce compounds that yield the "Brett signature," aromas that have been termed mousy, horsy, and rodent cage litter.

Brettanomyces are also easy to detect, and the most popular methods exploit their insensitivity to Acti-Dione™. There are other brewery contaminants that also are insensitive to Acti-Dione (e.g., *Candida* and *Hansenula*), but they are not nearly as common as *Brettanomyces*.

To detect *Brettanomyces*, prepare petri dishes with wort agar as described in the Slant Preparation and Inoculation section, adding 30 milligrams per liter Acti-Dione. After this media is autoclaved, the Acti-Dione level will drop into the 5–15 milligrams per liter range. Inoculate approximately 0.1 gram of yeast on the plate, using the procedures described in the Propagation section. Hold the plates at 77–86 °F (25–30 °C) for seven to ten days, then examine for growth.

Vino Strains: These yeast are indigenous to fruit and can be found throughout the Temperate Zone. Microbiological test results of the ambient air collected from several breweries in North America suggest that these yeasts are everywhere. Numerous chemical tests (i.e., tests involving growth media) are used to detect wild yeasts (Casey and Ingledew 1981, 1982), but they all have two shortfalls: (1) they support the growth of some strains but retard others; and (2) to date, all of the media used are unnatural to beer, which raises a concern that such media are capable of supporting microbes totally irrelevant to beer. Consequently, we do not think that current media plating procedures are effective in monitoring the presence of wild yeasts.

As an alternative, we found stressed fermentations to be useful. The procedure is exactly the same as the one used to detect superattenuators, except normal wort is used. A liter-sized all-malt brew, with an original gravity of 10 °P (1.040) and BUs around 10 milligrams per liter, is produced. At the end of the ferment, carefully decant the sediment from the sample, cool to 50 °F (10 °C), then taste. Since the fermentation temperature is 77 °F (25 °C), the sample will be estery. However, if vino strains are present, these will take on nail polish/solvent tones. Vino strains are furious producers of fusel alcohols, especially phenol alcohols like tyrosol and tryptophol, which have characteristic harsh phenolic flavors. In addition, vino strains invariably lead to elevated phenol tones that have characteristic Band-Aid/clove/medicinal tones.

Fermentation and Maturation

FERMENTATION BY-PRODUCTS

The primary by-products of fermentation are ethyl alcohol and carbon dioxide. In addition, there are other by-products that are minor in terms of concentration but major in terms of impact on beer flavor. For example, a beer with an alcohol level of 4% by weight (i.e., 4 grams per 100 grams) and a SG of 1.010 will have an alcohol concentration of 40,400 milligrams per liter. On the other hand, diacetyl, a minor by-product, can normally be detected in beer at concentrations of 0.1–0.2 milligram per liter. Even minor deviations from major metabolic pathways can impact beer flavor.

Stylistic considerations dictate which fermentation by-products are acceptable and which are not. This section focuses on identifying these by-products and the conditions that lead to their formation, as well as ways to reduce their concentrations, if and when appropriate.

Fusel Alcohols

Fusel alcohol, fusel oil, and higher alcohol are equivalent names for families of alcohol whose molecular structures are more complicated than that of ethyl alcohol. Fusel alcohols tend to be more intoxicating than ethyl alcohol and, in fact, more toxic as well. While they tend to be highly significant in brandy and other spirits, they are almost universally regarded as being incompatible with beer.

These are two types of fusel alcohols: aliphatic and phenol. Aliphatic alcohols have a straight line structure and are relatively volatile (Fix, *Zymurgy* 1993, 16:3). They tend to have warming alcohol-like flavors with fruity tones, mixed with others that recall solvents.

They lead to a definite harshness in beer aftertaste. Phenol alcohols are involatile, aromatic alcohols that have a bitter, medicinal flavor, sometimes mixed with roselike undertones.

Fusel alcohols differ from ethyl alcohol in that fusel alcohols are metabolized from amino acids rather than from sugars. As a consequence, yeast strains differ dramatically in their propensity for creating fusel alcohols. In particular, noncultured yeast as well as mutated culture yeast tend to produce far more fusel alcohols than standard brewing yeast (illustrated in table 3.1). The data in table 3.1 were obtained from test brews using worts of a standard sugar concentration (12 °P [1.048]). The yeast strains (with the exception of wild yeast) are those found in the Strains section of chapter 2.

Table 3.1 Fusel Alcohol Levels

Yeast Strain	Beer Type	Aliphatic Alcohols mg/L (threshold = 40–130)	Phenol Alcohols mg/L (threshold = 10–80)
Ballantine/Chico	Ale	70	30
Whitbread	Ale	138	60
W-206	Lager	25	15
W-34/70	Lager	35	18
Wild yeast	Ale	265	310

Table 3.1 and similar data (see Chen 1978) demonstrate that the dominant mechanisms leading to the formation of fusel alcohols are yeast strain and yeast purity. There are, however, other issues. Fermentation temperature is also important, particularly with lager strains. The data for W-206 and W-34/70 were taken from fermentations at 50 °F (10 °C). At 68 °F (20 °C), fusel levels will be much higher. Wort gravity is also an issue, as fusel levels tend to increase with gravity. This effect becomes particularly striking for worts with sugar contents of 16% (16 °P [1.065]) or higher. A closely related defect is an elevated wort amino acid pool, which can arise from high wort gravities and/or excess protein breakdown in malting or mashing. Excess amino acids are converted in part to fusel alcohols. Nevertheless, as the data in table 3.1 show, wild yeast contamination tends to have the most deleterious effects.

Closely related to phenol alcohols are other types of phenolic compounds that appear during beer fermentation. They also have medicinal flavoring, and the issues associated with them are almost identical to those associated with phenol alcohols. One exception to this is four-vinyl guaiacol levels in wheat beers that arise when selected wheat beer strains are used (Fix, *Principles of Brewing Science* 1989). Here, a soft clovelike tone is present without harsh medicinal undertones. However, a great deal of care is needed in working with these strains since minor mutations can have deleterious effects. This is perhaps why a Texas brewery famous for its Belgian-style wheat beer propagates fresh yeast from slants for every brew. Fermentation temperatures are also important with phenolic compounds, and those higher than the optimal temperatures (cited in chapter 2) can lead to an unmistakable Band-Aid-like flavor.

Esters

A strong case can be made that esters are the most important fermentation by-product. Indeed, all the major beer styles, including delicate ones like today's American lagers, have selected esters at or above threshold. Nonalcohol beers produced with yeast strains like *Saccharomyces ludwigie* tend to have very low ester levels (in addition to low alcohol levels). This has often been cited as the reason they tend to taste like hopped ice tea rather than beer.

Positive flavor tones that result from selected esters include a subtle fruitiness sometimes accompanied with complex and sophisticated undertones that recall specific fruits. For example, amyl acetate at or slightly above threshold gives a gentle hint of bananas (Fix, *Principles of Brewing Science* 1989). On the other hand, ethyl acetate at similar levels tends to recall a spectrum of fruit tones. Unfortunately, there is a negative to all of this. At too high a level and/or when produced under undesirable circumstances, esters can lead to flavors (taste and smell) that recall nail polish or other solvents.

Table 3.2 Ester Levels

Yeast Strain mg/L (threshold = 35)	Ethyl Acetate mg/L (threshold = 2)	Amyl Acetate
Ballantine/Chico	26	2
Whitbread	36	8
W-206	30	2
W-34/70	20	1

As with fusel alcohols, ester levels are profoundly affected by the type of yeast used (Fix 1987). The data in table 3.2 were obtained from the same fermentations used in table 3.1. The data explain in part why the different yeast strain groupings described in chapter 2 produce such dramatically different beers.

Ester levels increase with wort sugar levels in a superlinear manner, wort gravity is also a factor. This is why beers produced from high-gravity brewing systems, even after dilution, tend to have higher ester levels than equivalent beers brewed by a standard batch process.

Fermentation temperature is particularly critical, as ester levels decrease sharply with decreasing temperature. This is illustrated in table 3.3. The data in table 3.3 for the lager strain W-206 are not uncommon for these strains. There is a very definite change in beer flavors when these yeasts are used at too high of a temperature. The same is true of ale strains, however, the data in table 3.3 illustrate a counterpoint: at too low a temperature, they can lose their ale characteristics. Beers produced under such circumstances typically lack ale characteristics, but at the same time, they lack certain crucial lager characteristics as well. Some of the anemic pseudolager beers made with ale strains in the United Kingdom illustrate this point.

Table 3.3 Ester Levels of Yeast Strains at Different Fermentation Temperatures

Temperature °F (°C)	Ethyl Acetate (mg/L)	Amyl Acetate (mg/L)
Ballantine/Chico		
60 (16)	16	0.5
68 (20)	26	2.0
75 (24)	53	4.0
W-206		
50 (10)	30	2.0
68 (20)	92	8.0

Another important factor in ester formation is wort aeration, as yeast respiration competes with ester formation (Fix, *Principles of Brewing Science* 1989). Yeast pitched into worts with inadequate dissolved oxygen can lead to elevated ester levels, particularly the unpleasant solventlike ones. Table 3.4 illustrates this for the lager strain W-34/70 pitched into 13.5 °P wort at 50 °F (10 °C) (Schmidt 1995).

Table 3.4 Wort O_2 Levels Versus Beer Ester Levels

Wort O_2 (mg/L)	Ethyl Acetate (mg/L)	Amyl Acetate (mg/L)
8–10	15	0.5
6–8	24	1.0
4–6	30	2.0
2–4	45	3.0
0–2	62	4.0

Diacetyl

This carbonyl has become one of the most feared beer fermentation by-products. It has been estimated that flavors from diacetyl are responsible for the demise of more commercial breweries than all other beer off-flavors combined. This has particularly been the case in the last few decades, and this period has seen a definite shift in consumer tolerance of residual diacetyl in beer. Previously, many small breweries in the United States, the United Kingdom, and in Germany were able to survive in spite of elevated diacetyl levels, because their beers were the only fresh beers available. The locals were accustomed to the flavors and considered them to be natural to beer. As alternatives became available, consumer attitudes changed, with new products considered to be "cleaner." It is likely that the average consumer's shift in attitude was highly subjective and not based on discrimintaing beer analysis. Nevertheless, these were remarkable, worldwide attitude changes. (See Wainwright 1973 for an excellent survey of this subject.)

In fresh beer, diacetyl at or slightly above its threshold of 0.1 milligram per liter is often confused with flavors associated with caramel malts. Triangle tests (see Evaluating Flavor in chapter 6) with representative groups of beer drinkers illustrate this point. Typically, one-quarter to a one-third of the participants are unable to correctly identify fresh beers containing diacetyl at the 0.25 milligram per liter level from similar beers having light caramel malt charges in the 5–10% range. Diacetyl is highly unstable, and as beer ages, diacetyl-related flavors tend to take on very definite butter/butterscotch tones that become progressively raunchy in time. They are then easily detectable, even by unsophisticated beer drinkers, and are almost universally rejected.

Diacetyl in beer stems from a number of different mechanisms (Fix, *Brewing Techniques* 1993, 1:2). Selected gram-positive rods and cocci can create copious amounts of diacetyl, which quickly take on rancid butter tones. Equipment and pitching yeast are likely sources of such bacteria. Open fermenters located in less than ideal environments are notorious havens for gram-positive microbes. Poorly engineered breweries, especially their piping systems, are also culprits. In modern breweries, infected pitching yeast is the most likely source of diacetyl. Infections typically start out at low, insignificant levels, only to grow during repitching. Growth during yeast storage is of particular concern. Fortunately, such infections are readily detected at low levels by the procedures discussed previously in chapter 2.

Defects other than infection are also responsible for diacetyl flavors in beer. Brewing strains have the enzyme systems needed to create diacetyl from precursors like acetolactic acids, and these strains also have the enzymes necessary to reduce the diacetyl so formed into flavor-neutral compounds. When yeasts are reused, they start to change, and it is common for yeasts to gradually lose their capacity for fully reducing diacetyl in fermenting wort. The extreme case of full mutation can be checked by analysis (see Evaluating Pitching Yeast in chapter 2), but brewers should detect anomalies well before this happens. In this respect, a brewer's own palate is the only reliable tool for detecting small changes in pitching yeast. Successful brewers typically have developed a strong sensitivity to the flavor of diacetyl and can detect it well before average beer drinkers.

Diacetyl can also be a problem if the brewer prematurely separates beer and yeast before all the diacetyl formed is reduced to appropriately low levels. Also, a premature temperature reduction can sometimes have the same effect. Because metabolic activity of active yeast cells is the only viable way to reduce diacetyl, these situations will cause diacetyl to spill over into the finished beer at detectable levels.

Another phenomenon that is not uncommon is for diacetyl flavors to suddenly appear in packaged beer (bottles or kegs). In this circumstance, diacetyl precursors spill over into the beer and then oxidize into diacetyl. This is a nonenzymatic reaction that requires only the presence of oxygen (Ibid.).

Wort that is deficient in key amino acids, most notably valine, tends to promote diacetyl in finished beer (Ibid.). Fortunately, all-malt worts are typically rich in amino acids, so deficiencies arise only in unusual formulations that use high fractions of unmalted materials as carbohydrate sources.

Acetaldehyde

Acetaldehyde, also a carbonyl, is the precursor to ethanol in the major fermentative pathway (Fix, *Principles of Brewing Science* 1989). Most brewing strains reduce just about all of it to ethanol, so residuals usually are well below its threshold of 8–10 milligrams per liter. Indeed, data given in Piendl's "Bier aus alles Welt" columns (Piendl 1970–1990), show that almost all the world's major commercial beers have acetaldehyde levels in the range of 1–3 milligrams per liter. One striking exception is the largest selling beer in the United States that has a level in the 7–9 milligrams per liter range. In this beer, acetaldehyde leaves a rather snappy, freshly cut green apple tone, most likely because the beer is kraeusened and has a very brief maturation period.

Acetaldehyde is also formed from infections involving *Zymomonas*. This gram-negative bacteria is highly sensitive to halogen sanitizers (chlorine and iodine in particular), therefore it is rarely present in operating breweries. Various strains have been isolated in soil and can be a problem for breweries where construction work is going on. Although most strains of *Zymomonas* are short-lived, they are very dangerous and can create various obnoxious products in beer within a few hours. Most notable of these is acetaldehyde, which in this circumstance tends to have an unmistakable rotten apple tone.

Sulfur Compounds

These are the least understood of the fermentation by-products, possibly because most have lower thresholds than carbonyl compounds. Hydrogen sulfide is possibly the best understood by-product and is naturally produced and reduced in the fermenter. The flavor threshold of hydrogen sulfide is in the range of 10–35 milligrams per liter (i.e., parts per billion), and it tends to impart sulfury tones that recall rotten eggs.

Figure 3.1 shows that there are typically several hydrogen sulfide peaks during fermentation. Studies show that hydrogen sulfide levels

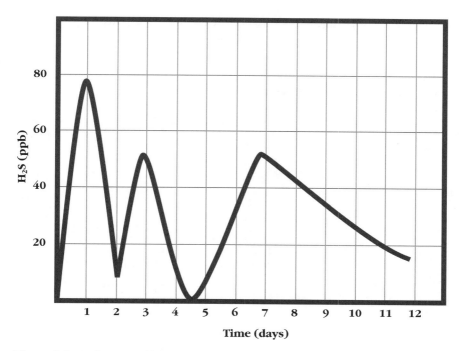

Figure 3.1. Hydrogen sulfide curve with lager strain W34/70 at 46 °F (8 °C).

tend to decrease with both chilled wort dissolved oxygen levels and wort trub levels (Nagami 1980). Yeast growth tends to promote hydrogen sulfide, and both can be controlled by applying carbon dioxide counterpressure during fermentation. Finally, large amounts of autolyzed yeast at the fermentation end point can lead to the formation of many sulfur products, and even brief maturation periods promote its removal.

Most gram-negative bacteria relevant to beer are strong sulfur producers. While these microbes tend to be short-lived, the products they produce have an obnoxious habit of surviving. This is true for *Escherichia coli* and other wort spoilers, as well as for *Pectinatus*, *Megasphaeria*, and other anaerobic rods found in the latter stages of brewing. In each case, unpleasant sulfur tones recalling rotten vegetables are usually detectable.

As noted in chapter 2, different yeast strains tend to have different capacities for reducing sulfur products. This is somewhat complicated by the fact that higher temperatures in ale fermentation (as opposed to lagers) also tend to promote the reduction of sulfur compounds. Table 3.5 provides selected data taken from Owades and

Plam (1988). The pattern is typical in that ales have a lower DMS content than lagers. Also, sulfur levels in infected beer tend to be intolerably high.

Table 3.5 Sulfur Compounds in Beer

Sulfur Compound	Threshold (ppb)	British Porter	German Lager	Infected Beer
Ethyl mercaptan	2	0.75	0.39	nd
Dimethyl sulfide	30	nd	40.00	92
Dimethyl disulfide	7	0.52	nd	4

FERMENTATION VESSELS

The last two decades have seen a major switch from traditional two-vessel fermentation and maturation setups to unitanks, where fermentation and aging are done in a single vessel. This resulted in changes in vessel geometry. Both impact finished beer quality.

Nathan first proposed the unitank in 1908, and his 1927 patented unitank had all the essential features, including a conical bottom (see Nathan 1927, 1930). He was not motivated by economic considerations, but rather by his desire to protect beer from the hostile, bacteria-ridden environments prevalent in his time. He even made provisions for wort cooling to be done in the unitank, with cold break removal via the conical bottom.

His ideas fell on deaf ears until the 1960s when Vacaro designed a large unitank system for the Rainier Brewery in Seattle, Washington (Larson and Brandon 1988). His design permitted breweries to make major increases in their production capacity, at a fraction of the traditional cost of such an expansion. Not surprisingly, the idea caught on, and unitanks have become common in both large and small breweries.

De Clerck, who was acquainted with Nathan's designs and ideas, did a serious study of fermenter geometry (de Clerck 1957). He concluded that the optimal shape would limit fermenter depth to the 1–2-meter range. Shallow "wading pool" open fermenters are examples of de Clerck's criterion, but such fermenters have largely disappeared. However, the Anchor Brewery in San Francisco, California, uses such a fermenter for its steam beer. In general, shallow open fermenters were replaced with horizontal, cylindrical closed vessels.

     An Analysis of Brewing Techniques

While different in shape, both the open and closed fermenters have large surface areas relative to their depths.

One of the objectives of the unitank was space conservation. It is common to define a unitank's effective height to diameter ratio by the lambda (λ) (figure 3.2). A recent study found that best results are obtained in designs where λ is less than or equal to one (Unterstein 1994).

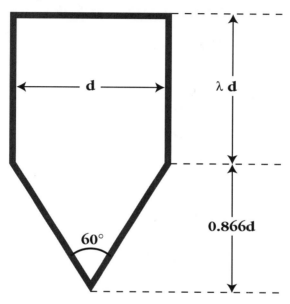

Figure 3.2. Effective height to diameter ratio using λ.

To test these ideas, we did some trial ferments in the tall fermenter and in the squat fermenter shown in figure 3.3. Approximately 20% head space was used, which led to a height to diameter liquid ratio of 3.0 for the tall vessel and 0.67 for the squat vessel. The major difference in the two was that the results obtained with the tall fermenter were inconsistent—some trials were normal, others were erratic. Yeast strains also influenced results in that some strains were strongly affected by geometry, while some were not. Table 3.6 shows some of our test results. Given this data, we agree with Unterstein (1994)—that the (effective) height should be less than the fermenter diameter. In these trial ferments, an all-malt wort with an original gravity of 1.048 was used, with the W-34/70 yeast strain, and fermentation temperature of 46 °F (8 °C).

A number of studies help explain why fermenter geometry is important. Knudsen (1978) did a careful study of tank hydraulics and found that carbon dioxide gradients were present, with the largest values near the bottom of the tank. This led to the development of a heterogeneous flow field that included isolated vortices. A typical pattern is shown in figure 3.4. The maximum vortex formation occurred at the top of the tank, and heterogeneities increased with the height to diameter ratio. In such cases, there are also gradients in temper-

Figure 3.3. A squat tank and a Zahm and Nagel no. 5 tank.

ature, sugar concentration, pH, and other key variables. In effect, tall fermenters have not one but several different types of fermentation taking place in parallel.

Table 3.6 Trial Ferments

Criterion	Tall Fermenter	Squat Fermenter
Fermentation time (days)	10.000	8.000
Final gravity	1.010	1.011
Diacetyl (mg/L)	0.350	0.060
Clearing	Poor	Excellent
pH end point	4.600	4.400

Several approaches have been taken in designing relatively tall fermenters where these gradients will not exist. In small research versions (one barrel or less in volume), the most cost-effective approach uses stirring devices inside the fermenter. These stirring devices have also been used in large fermenters, such as the agitated batch system developed by the Schlitz Brewing Company (now part of Stroh's Brewing Company).

In Europe, there has been some interest in recirculating systems (Annemüller and Manger 1995), originally for economic reasons. Instead of cooling the contents of an entire tank, a recirculating volume of approximately 5–7% is cooled. Fermentations done in prototypes (see figure 3.5) show that a uniform temperature can be maintained in a recirculating system at a fraction of the cost associated

An Analysis of Brewing Techniques

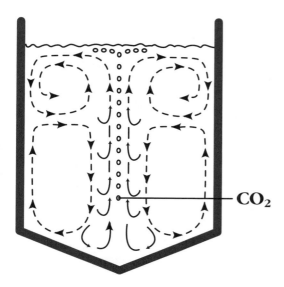

CO_2

Figure 3.4. Tank hydraulics.

with tanks using cooling jackets. In addition, recirculation has the unexpected benefit of removing the fermentative inconsistencies associated with tall fermenters. The reduction in end point diacetyl levels is particularly striking.

There is considerable evidence that the cleanest, best-tasting beers are made (all other things being equal) when fermentation takes place in an open fermenter (housed in a protected environment), and when maturation is done in a closed vessel under moderate carbon dioxide counterpressure. We did a number of trial brews to test these points, using the 50-liter unitank shown in figure 3.5. The following three configurations were used:

(1) Open fermentation: The lid to the unitank was removed during the first 90% of the fermentation. Fermented beer was then transferred to tanks, like those in figure 3.3, for maturation.

(2) Closed fermentation: Same as open fermentation except the lid to the unitank was clamped tight, and a carbon dioxide bleed from the tank's top was used.

(3) Unitank operation: Here, fermentation and maturation took place in the tank, with yeast being removed from the cone after the end of the fermentation.

Fermentation and Maturation

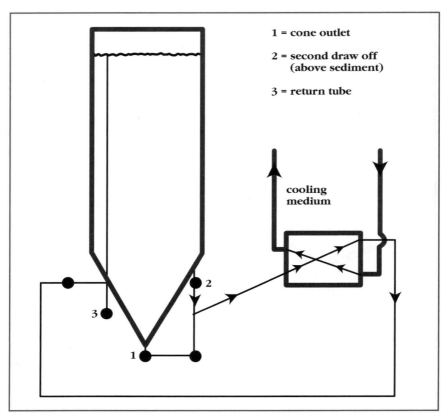

1 = cone outlet

2 = second draw off
(above sediment)

3 = return tube

cooling
medium

Figure 3.5. A recirculating unitank.

Nothing in the data collected (gravity, pH, diacetyl levels, etc.) distinguished any of the three methods. Nevertheless, a blind taste test revealed a preference for open fermentation over closed as well as closed over the unitank operation.

Cleaning
and Sanitation

An effective and rational cleaning program for brewing equipment is the brewer's main line of defense against beer-spoiling infection. Inconsistency in a cleaning program has a pernicious way of leading to inconsistency in beer quality. We cannot emphasize enough that it is impossible to properly sanitize equipment that is not clean. Residual films and soils tend to degrade the effectiveness of most sanitizers, and residual organic material can serve as a future food source for microbes once the effect of the sanitizer dissipates.

The two major targets of cleaning are: (1) organic material, including proteins, fatty compounds, hop residues from wort or beer, and biofilms consisting of yeast and/or bacteria; and (2) inorganic material, including beer stone (gray/brown films of calcium oxalate) as well as residuals from detergents used to remove organic soils.

CLEANING AGENTS

Two entirely different compounds are needed to clean these materials. Detergents are the most effective means of removing organic soils, while sequestering agents are best for inorganic materials.

Here is a popular, five-step cleaning method:

(1) Preclean by rinsing with cold water. (Hot water has a tendency to fuse organic soils to the surface, making it harder to remove them in the next stage.)
(2) Wash with detergent to remove organic soils.
(3) Rinse with hot water.

(4) Sequester to remove inorganic film.

(5) A final rinse with warm water.

Detergents

There are four relevant aspects of detergents:

(1) Surfactance is a measure of a detergent's "wetting power." Detergents are surfactants in that they are surface active. Their molecules have a hydrophilic (water-loving) head and a hydrophobic (water-hating) tail. The goal is to reduce the surface tension of organic soils on equipment. This, plus an appropriate amount of mechanical agitation (i.e., pressure sprays), leads to the removal of organic dirt on equipment surfaces. The detergents cited in table 4.1 are rated *(A)* through *(C)* with respect to surfactance; *(A)* denotes the most effective, *(C)* the least effective. It should be noted that *(C)* detergents can be just as effective as *(A)* agents, but more time and mechanical agitation are needed. The *(C)* detergents are typically less hazardous.

(2) Emulsification/saponification is a measure of a detergent's ability to break down fats and oils into smaller units that are more easily removed during rinsing. Ratings are from *(A)* to *(C)*.

(3) Rinsability is a measure of rinsing ease. Some detergents leave stubborn, inorganic films that require serious sequestering. These are *(C)* rated. Others come off with simple water rinses and are *(A)* rated.

(4) Precautions vary greatly with respect to safety issues when using detergents. Those with high precaution ratings require maximal protection, including protective gloves, goggles, and protective clothing. A medium rating requires protective gloves, while a low rating requires only common-sense usage. Careful brewers will nevertheless want to be conservative, which suggests wearing goggles with medium-rated detergents and protective gloves with all detergents.

Table 4.1 lists the major detergents relevant to brewing. The strength of powdered detergents is measured in kilograms per 100 liters (i.e., percent on a weight to volume basis), and that of liquid detergents is percent on a liquid basis (i.e., liters per 100 liters).

Detergents based on weak alkali and active oxygen are finding widespread acceptance in commercial and amateur brewing. Active oxygen

Table 4.1 Detergent Ratings

Agent	Strength	Temperature °F (°C)	Sur-fac-tance	Emul-sifica-tion	Rins-ability	Precaution Level
PBW* (buffered alkali with active oxygen)	1-3	122-140 (50-60)	A	A	A	Low
Caustic (sodium hydroxide)	1-3	122-140 (50-60)	A	B	C	High
TSP (trisodium phosphate)	5	140-158 (60-70)	B	B	C	Medium
Washing soda (sodium carbonate/ sodium silicate)	5	140-158 (60-70)	C	B	C	Low
B-brite (sodium percarbonate/sodium silicate)	5	140-158 (60-70)	C	C	C	Low
Vinegar	50	212 (100)	C	B	A	High

(A) is very effective, (C) is least effective, and (B) is somewhere in between.
*PBW is a trade name of Five Star Products of Commerce City Company.

enhances the surfactance and emulsification of weak alkali, such as sodium metasilicate, creating a detergent that is as strong as a caustic but not as hazardous and one with better rinsability. The first such product, PBW™, should not to be confused with older, weaker combined cleaners/sanitizers using sodium percarbonate. We want to emphasize that PBW is formulated strictly as a cleaning agent, not as a combined cleaner and sanitizer.

Among traditional cleaners, caustics are the strongest, but they are also the most hazardous. Recommendations have called for caustic solutions to be near a temperature of 212 °F (100 °C), but this temperature is of dubious value. First, mixing sodium hydroxide and water at 212 °F (100 °C) results in an exothermic reaction, and the hazardous nature of such solutions is extreme. We found that by lowering the temperature to the 122-140 °F (50-60 °C) range, little is lost in terms of strength, and a much safer product is obtained. Nevertheless, all precautions should be taken when working with caustics. Trisodium phosphate and various washing sodas offer weaker yet less hazardous alternatives, and both have long and excellent track records in brewing. Vinegar is a special case; in general, it is not as effective as alkali cleaners. However, there is one major exception: at high temperatures—as close to 212 °F (100 °C) as possible—vinegar is very effective for cleaning various films from copper equipment. Vinegar itself is not hazardous and, in fact, is quite natural to beer. The high precaution rating stems from the high temperature.

We want to emphasize that more serious brewing accidents occur from the spilling of hot liquids than from all toxic cleaners and sanitizers combined.

Sequestering Agents

Phosphoric acid is a proven sequestering agent in the brewing industry. It is a weak organic acid that is natural to beer. While it is adequate for preventing the buildup of beer stone, it lacks the strength to remove preexisting beer stone. In such cases, nitric acid, a strong and hazardous acid, can be used. There are some new and interesting sequestering agents that are a blend of phosphoric and nitric acid. These are not as hazardous as the latter, and they can be used at lower temperatures than phosphoric acid sequestering agents. Table 4.2 provides additional information about the major sequestering agents.

Table 4.2 Sequestering Agents

Agent	Strength (%)	Temperature °F (°C)	Sequestering Power	Rins- ability	Precaution Level
Phosphoric acid	1–5	120 (50)	B	A	Medium
Vinegar	50–100	120–140 (50–60)	C	A	Low
Nitric acid	1–2	68 (20)	A	B	High
Phosphoric–nitric acid blends	1–2	77–86 (25–30)	A	A	Medium

SANITIZERS

In brewing, sanitation means lowering microbe levels to levels where residual microbes will not affect beer quality. Sterilization, on the other hand, is the total eradication of microbes. The effectiveness of sanitizing solutions depends on the following key parameters:

- Concentration (or, in the case of thermal sanitation, temperature)
- Type of microbe present
- Contact time

Given the first two, the D-value of a sanitizing solution is the time it takes (in minutes) to reduce the microbial level by a factor of at least ten. For example, a D-value of five minutes is typical of many sanitizing solutions. This means that a contact time of $1 \times 5 = 5$ reduces the microbial level by a factor of ten. A contact time of two

D-values, like 2 x 5 = 10 minutes, gives a reduction factor of 10 x 10 = 100. A contact time of 3 x 5 = 15 minutes gives a total reduction factor of 10 x 10 x 10 = 1,000. For D-values above five, proportionally longer times are needed and vice versa. The general relationship is

$$N(t) = N_0 \ 10^{-t/D}$$

where *N(t)* is the number of microbes remaining after t minutes contact time, N_0 is the initial microbial level, and *D* is the D-value.

The question of how many D-values are required for proper sanitation is difficult to answer because it depends on the cleanliness of the equipment to be sanitized. If a rigorous cleaning program is in place, experience shows that a microbial reduction by a factor of one thousand is adequate.

The type of microbe present is also a major factor. For example, most sanitizing solutions have very low D-values associated with gram-negative bacteria like *Escherichia coli*, while the D-values needed for more resistant gram-positive bacteria are much higher. Invariably, contact times quoted by sanitizer manufacturers are for *Escherichia coli*, and those times are likely to be inadequate for general brewery use.

Iodophors—Iodine-based halogen sanitizers are the most popular in North American breweries. The iodine is bound up with a high molecule weight carrier, and the resulting mixture is called an iodophor. Like chlorine and other halogen sanitizers, iodophors display a wide range of activity against beer-spoiling microbes. In addition, a decrease in sanitizing power is indicative of a loss of color, hence, this is easy to monitor. At the levels recommended in table 4.3, iodophors are not harmful to stainless steel equipment, but at elevated levels, solutions can stain. They will stain plastic at virtually any concentration.

There are two basic versions of iodophor available today. One type has iodine bound up with an acid. The most widely used in brewing is an iodine and phosphoric acid blend. This iodophor has several advantages: (1) phosphoric acid is a weak acid, natural to beer; (2) it also works as a sequestering agent; and (3) phosphoric acid helps counteract high water pH (Block 1991). The major disadvantage with an iodine and phosphoric acid blend is that it creates a lot of foam.

In the other version, iodine is bound up with antifoaming agents, such as lanolin or fatty acids derived from alcohol. Because the carriers in these iodophors are potentially destructive to beer foam, they are not widely used in commercial brewing. However, they are popular with amateur brewers. Experience shows that if equipment is properly rinsed after use, antifoaming iodophors are reasonable alternatives to foaming iodophors. Care must be taken with water pH used with these iodophors, and again, the color of the sanitizing solution should be monitored. A dark yellow color indicates the presence of an active sanitizer.

It is not uncommon to see contact times of two minutes recommended for iodophors. Practical brewing experience shows that this is inadequate, especially with selected spore-forming yeast (Ibid.). We found that the D-values in table 4.3 are adequate for a wide range of bacteria and yeasts.

Table 4.3 D-values for Iodophors

Strength (% mg/L)	D-value (minutes)
0.078 (12.5 ppm free iodine)	5
0.156 (25.0 ppm free iodine)	3

Note: A contact time of three D-values means that 5 x 3 = 15 minutes are needed for the 0.078% solution while 3 x 3 = 9 minutes are needed for the 0.156% solution.

Two points are important to keep in mind. First, the D-values quoted in tables 4.3, 4.4, and 4.5 refer to solutions at ambient temperatures. The sanitizing power of iodophors deteriorates as temperatures increase beyond ambient. In fact, at temperatures much above 140 °F (60 °C), toxic fumes are a possibility. And second, D-values of iodine actually start increasing once the 25 ppm level of free iodine is reached (Ibid.). In addition, such solutions are capable of staining even stainless equipment, which means too much is bad as far as iodophor is concerned.

Peracetic Acid—This sanitizer was first introduced in Germany (Schröder 1984) where brewers have traditionally preferred natural cleaning and sanitation agents. Peracetic acid, a blend of acetic acid and hydrogen peroxide, certainly qualifies as being natural to beer. It is a strong oxidizing agent, and unlike halogen sanitizers (i.e., chlorine and iodine), it is highly aggressive against all forms of spore-forming yeast. In fact, peracetic acid comes as close to being biocidal (i.e., a sterilizer) as any sanitizing agent in current use. Unfortunately, its strong oxidizing power makes it highly hazardous to human skin. After decades of successful use in Europe, it is now being introduced

An Analysis of Brewing Techniques

into North American brewing (Lenahan 1992). It is well suited for highly automated cleaning in place systems, but not necessarily for smaller operations where manual applications are used. However, a procedure that is finding favor in small operations is using an iodophor for everyday sanitizing and peracetic acid periodically (e.g., once every five sanitizing sessions), under careful supervision. Our tests indicate this method is just as effective as using peracetic acid exclusively. We also found that peracetic acid can be used on virtually any equipment (metallic or otherwise) that is noncorrosive.

Table 4.4 D-values for Peracetic Acid

Strength (%)	D-value (minutes)
0.2	1.0
0.5	0.5

Note: The rule that three D-values is sufficient for clean equipment amounts to 3 x 0.5 = 1.5 minutes for the 0.5% solution, while 3 x 1 = 3 minutes is needed for the 0.2% solution.

Quaternary Ammonium Compounds (Quats)—These agents were popularized by de Clerck (1957), and they have a number of advantages. Quats are insensitive to pH, noncorrosive, nonirritating, and they have low toxicity. They are particularly aggressive against all known gram-positive microbes, and their D-values are comparable to those for peracetic acid. Ironically, the D-values for wort-spoiling, gram-negative bacteria are magnitudes higher. This means that if quats are used to sanitize wort cooling equipment, long contact times are required. De Clerck suggests soaking equipment overnight. Quats definitely must be rinsed after application, which takes some effort as their rinsability is even lower than iodophors that contain antifoam constituents.

Table 4.5 D-values for Quats

Strength (%)	D-value for Gram-Negative Bacteria	D-value for Gram-Positive Bacteria
0.25	30	5
0.50	25	1

Note: A contact time of three D-values amounts to 1 x 3 = 3 minutes for the 0.50% solution to counteract gram-positive bacteria. This increases rather dramatically to 25 x 3 = 75 minutes to counteract gram-negative bacteria.

Chlorine—Chlorine gas has traditionally been the large brewer's sanitizer of choice. Chlorinated liquid solutions (e.g., household bleach, which is 5.25% sodium hypochlorite) have also been widely used in brewing. However, in recent years their use has decreased dramatically. One reason is that chlorine tends to be more harmful to metals than other alternatives. A more serious concern is that some microbes display a strong resistance to chlorinated solutions, even at high concentrations and long contact times (Sorensen, de Verno, and Lord 1983). (The same is true of other halogen sanitizers.) Microbes resistant to chlorine include gram-positive bacteria, such as *Pediococcus damnosus,* which are common brewery contaminants (Sorensen, de Verno, and Lord 1983). For example, we have found that a 1% solution of household bleach is a suitable sanitizer for the plastic tubing used in wort cooling. At this stage in brewing, gram-negative bacteria are the greatest danger, and these microbes are highly sensitive to chlorine, with associated D-values under one minute. At later stages of brewing, peracetic acid or quats are preferred for tubing.

Alcohols—These are well-suited sanitizers for yeast work. (See Propagation and Slant Preparation and Inoculation in chapter 2.) Ironically, they are biocidal against most microbes but totally ineffective against some spore-forming organisms. This is why we recommend that inoculation loops first be flamed (see chapter 2). After that, storing them in alcohol is adequate.

The sanitizing strength of alcohols increases with their molecular structure. Simple alcohols like methyl alcohol are totally ineffective, while the "higher" isopropyl alcohol is widely used. We found ethyl alcohol to be almost as good, especially when spiked with a 1% phosphoric acid charge (and it is totally natural to beer). Without the presence of water, alcohols will not denature selected proteins, which is why the most common isopropyl solutions are at 70% strength. Pure grain spirits are a commonly available source of ethyl alcohol, and we dilute these to 70–80% strength with distilled water.

The D-values for alcohols vary tremendously depending on the type of microbe being attacked. Therefore, we consider alcohols to be excellent solutions for keeping previously sterilized equipment sterile, rather than using them as a sterilant or a sanitizer. Having a spray bottle on hand that is filled with an alcohol solution is also useful and convenient.

Heat—Dry heat, such as produced in an autoclave or a high-temperature pressure cooker, is the only guaranteed way to sterilize for microbes relevant to beer. The rule of 257 °F (125 °C) at 15 psi for fifteen minutes is sufficient.

Moist heat has long been viewed favorably by brewers as a totally natural sanitizer. It is also the most hazardous, particularly if near-boiling temperatures are used. This, plus a fear of resistant thermophilic lactic acid bacteria, has discouraged the widespread use of moist heat sterilization in modern brewing.

To evaluate the effectiveness of heat sanitation, a Z-value is used. This is the increase in °F needed to reduce the D-value by a factor of ten. The relevant formula is

$$D = D_0 \, 10^{-(t-140)/Z}$$

where Z is the Z-value, t the temperature in °F, and D_0 the D-value at 140 °F (60 °C). Representative values are given in table 4.6. Observe that the Z-value does not have units but does depend on the temperature scale used. Since the above formula is expressed in °F, the Z-values in table 4.6 use these units. Note that a temperature change of 18 °F is equal to a temperature change of

$$18 \times (5/9) = 10 \text{ °C.}$$

Table 4.6 D- and Z-values for Thermal Sanitation in Fahrenheit Units

Microbe Type	D-value (minutes)	Z-value
Brewers' yeast	1	18
Wild yeast	1	18
Thermophobic bacteria	5	18
Thermophilic bacteria	20	72

To cite a specific example, we shall show that holding a liquid at 140 °F (60 °C) for five minutes will reduce yeast counts by a factor of $10^5 = 100,000$. Indeed, from table 4.6 we get (for yeast)

$$D_0 = 1 \text{ minute, } Z = 18.$$

Hence the relevant D-value is

$$D = 1 \times 10^{-(140 - 140)/18} = 1 \text{ minute.}$$

The contact time of five minutes at 140 °F (60 °C) is therefore equal to five D-values, and hence the one hundred thousand reduction factor in yeast cell counts. An increase in temperature of 18 °F (which is the same as an increase of 10 °C) represents one Z-value and will reduce the D-value by a factor of ten (i.e., from one minute to six seconds). This means six seconds at 158 °F (70 °C) is equivalent to five D-values and will reduce the yeast count by a factor of at least one hundred thousand. Thermophilic bacteria, on the other hand, are far more resistant to heat. For example, ten minutes at 140 °F (60 °C) is only half a D-value and, hence, will lead to a microbial reduction by a factor of $10^{-5} = 3.2$. To get to the desired level of $10^5 = 100,000$, either more time or a higher temperature is needed. Since the D-value for thermophilic bacteria is twenty minutes, a total of $5 \times 20 = 100$ minutes is needed at 140 °F (60 °C). On the other hand, if the temperature is increased one Z-value, namely from 140 °F (60 °C) to $140 + 72 = 212$ °F (100 °C), then the resulting D-value will be reduced to $20 \div 10 = 2$ minutes. This means that a $5 \times 2 = 10$-minute contact time is needed to get the 10^5 reduction.

Miscellaneous—There are a variety of "quick and easy," "one-step" cleaners/sanitizers currently on the market. Most are based on percarbonates and were originally designed for winemakers, but they are also sold at many homebrewing outlets. We are not terribly impressed by them, nor are they used in commercial brewing. The margin for error in brewing is, after all, significantly lower than it is in winemaking.

5

Packaging Beer

FINING AGENTS

Various fining agents have been used in brewing for centuries. In today's breweries they are used in chill proofing and to remove yeast biomass.

Chill proofing: When beer is chilled there is a strong tendency for high molecular weight proteins and polyphenols to form a complex. This complex is usually insoluble at low temperatures and a colloidal haze forms. Fining agents are designed to remove either the large proteins or the large polyphenols, thereby reducing a beer's susceptibility to chill haze.

Yeast biomass: At the end of the fermentation there is still a large concentration of yeast in suspension, typically several million cells per milliliter, even with flocculent strains. Beer transfer to maturation tanks (or yeast removal from cones in unitanks) generally does not greatly affect the concentration of yeast in suspension. This biomass has a negative charge and can be removed with positively charged fining agents.

However, suspended yeast and colloidal haze are not the only sources of beer turbidity. Haze can also arise from a number of technical errors in brewing, such as the following:

(1) Selected nonculture yeast, bacteria, and mutated culture yeast can lead to a biological haze in beer.
(2) High molecular carbohydrates and gums, like beta-glucan, can be extracted during wort production (see Mashing Systems in chapter 1). If these constituents are present in beer at too high a level, they come out of solution and form what is known as a starch haze. This type of haze is easy to distinguish from chill haze, since it tends to be intractable and is present at all temperatures.

(3) As beer ages, staling invariably starts at some point, and this is contiguous with the formation of oxidation haze. This usually begins with a slight dullness and then slowly increases until flavor deteriorates.

(4) Various metals are strong catalysts for several inorganic haze-forming mechanisms. Copper and iron are common culprits. Consequently, it is best to keep iron levels in beer below 0.10 milligram per liter and copper below 0.15 milligram per liter. Traces of these metals can be extracted from brewing materials and equipment. However, experience shows that water is the most likely source of inorganic contamination.

We want to stress that the best way to remove haze that results from technical errors (versus from chill haze and suspended yeast) is to make appropriate changes in the brewing process—not by fining or filtration.

It is also important to emphasize that chill proofing is something of a double-edged sword. Over fining can negatively effect beer properties such as body, foam, and taste. An amazing example of this is hot-side aeration. Indeed, one of the best-known methods for removing high molecular weight polyphenols is to raise the mash to 158–176 °F (70–80 °C), then saturate it with oxygen (Morton and Sfat 1986). This dramatically reduces phenol content, and beers produced this way are typically immune to chill haze. However, this procedure also destroys the finished beer flavor profile, which is the main reason it is not used in practical brewing! While the methods we discussed are not nearly as destructive, each requires care in its use, because in beer fining, too much of a good thing is rarely good.

We used Formazin Turbidity units to measure haze levels in the samples tested. A visual description of these units is contained in table 5.1. The following procedure was used for each of the fining agents discussed in this section. After fining and normal beer maturation (six weeks) the samples were given a coarse 3-micron filtration, which typically resulted in less than 100 haze units. The beer was then anaerobically packaged in 12-ounce bottles, and samples that had air levels above 0.5 milliliter per 12 ounces were rejected. The beers were then stressed by storing for five days at 140 °F (60 °C), followed by two days at 32 °F (0 °C).

Samples were then classified according to the categories in table 5.1 (see *ASBC Methods of Analysis* 1992).

Table 5.1 Visual Description of Formazin Turbidity Units

Units	Haze Description
0	Brilliant
0-100	Very clear
100-200	Clear with slight dullness
200-300	See-through haze
> 400	Murky

We found that in small-scale brewing, fining procedures that yield 150-250 Formazin Turbidity Units in stressed beer are satisfactory. Values above 300 usually indicate defects, and values below 100 usually signal overfining and possible damage to other beer aspects.

Irish Moss

This is not a moss but a vegetable matter primarily composed of carrageen, a form of seaweed. Its gel strength and viscosity come from its 3,6-anhydrogalactose content, and its protein interaction capability comes from its ester sulfate fraction. Since Irish moss is purified by processing, different forms of it are not necessarily equivalent. It is generally available in flakes, in refined flakes, or in powder form. As a fining agent, Irish moss has three advantages: (1) it is truly a processing agent and not an ingredient, and, hence, it will not be present in finished beer, even at trace levels; (2) it is added during the boiling of wort, so it is a sterile fining procedure; and (3) if properly used, it is selective to haze-forming, high molecular weight protein.

To understand how fining works, we must first note that proteins are either negatively or positively charged. The two most important factors in determining the electrical charge of a protein are its amino acid structure and the pH of the substrate. The isoelectric point is the pH of the substrate at which the protein has no charge. If the pH of the medium is below the isoelectric point, the protein particle will have a positive charge, otherwise it will be negative. At a wort pH in the range of 5.0-5.5, haze-forming proteins generally have a positive charge (their isoelectric points are typically higher than 6.0). The reverse is true for Irish moss, in that it is negatively charged. This means it will electrically attract haze-forming proteins, and the complex will sediment and be removed from wort.

Irish moss, however, cannot be used indiscriminately. Desirable small- and medium-sized proteins have isoelectric points only slightly

below the wort pH. In practice, this means they are primarily negatively charged, but some may be positively charged. If too much Irish
moss is added, the excess will interact with the desirable proteins. As
with other agents, this may compromise beer foam and body. In addition, there is a special concern unique to kettle fining agents like Irish
moss: along with the undesirable reduction of wort FAN levels comes
the increased potential for dysfunctional fermentations. As a consequence, Irish moss is not recommended for protein-deficient worts.
Those produced from malt syrups are an example.

Table 5.2 gives the results from our test brews using refined Irish
moss flakes at various concentrations. (The usual homebrew concentration is 1 teaspoon per 5 gallons, which is 1/24 gram per liter.) We
found that different concentration levels did not affect the stability of
finished beer, nor did they offer chill proofing. Commercial concentrations are two to three times higher (1/16–1/8 gram per liter). We
found the top end was the best choice, however, any increase beyond
that had negative effects. (Test brew results with other forms of Irish
moss can be found in Fix, *Crosby and Baker Research Report,* 1993.)

Table 5.2 Fining Results of Irish Moss Test Brews

Concentration (g/L)	Formazin Turbidity Units	Form	Fermentation
1/24	350–400	Normal	Normal
1/12	200–250	Normal	Normal
1/8	150–200	Slightly below normal	Normal
1/4	100–150	Poor	Slow, high FG

Isinglass

This is another product from the ocean that has been used for centuries (Cowper and Taylor 1988; Mellon 1995). It comes from the
swim bladders of tropical fish and is one of the purest forms of collagen found in nature. Isinglass has long been considered an indis-
pensable fining agent for cask-conditioned ales, and it is finding favor
as a prefiltration aid on other beers. We found it to be an excellent
agent for reducing yeast biomass, however, its chill-proofing properties are weak. The latter is not an issue for cask-conditioned ales, but
other chill proofing agents need to be added for other beers.

Collagen consists of three amino acid units and has an isoelectric
point in the range of 5.0–5.5; thus, it is positively charged in beer (pH

An Analysis of Brewing Techniques

equals 4.0–4.5). Yeast are negatively charged, so isinglass is well suited for yeast settling. Table 5.3 gives our test brew results. Isinglass was added to fermented beer in aging tanks. The suspended yeast had a concentration of about one million cells per milliliter.

Table 5.3 Fining Results of Isinglass Test Brews

Isinglass (mg/L)	Suspended Yeast Cell Count (approximate)
0	1.00×10^6
15	$0.25–0.50 \times 10^6$
30	$0.15–0.25 \times 10^6$
60	$0.01–0.10 \times 10^6$

In cask-conditioned ales, a reduction of yeast cells by a factor of two to four is generally adequate, so isinglass concentrations around 15 milligrams per liter are used. Brewers who use isinglass as a pre-filtration aid generally use concentrations in the 30–60 milligrams per liter range.

Ready-to-use isinglass is available in liquid form, but it has not found acceptance among professional brewers. The general consensus is that best results are obtained with freshly prepared solutions, generally made thirty-six to forty-eight hours before use. To prepare an isinglass solution, use the following procedure:

(1) For dilution, the total amount of isinglass is dissolved in distilled water. The ratio of the volume of distilled water to the volume of beer to be fined is usually around 1/100. For example, if 1 hectoliter (100 liters) of beer is to be fined at a rate of 30 milligrams per liter, then 3 grams of isinglass are needed, and they are dissolved in 1 liter of distilled water.
(2) After dilution, lower the pH of the solution to the 2.5–3.0 range with a weak organic acid. (Citric, phosphoric, and tartaric acid are most commonly used.)
(3) Store solution at a temperature below 59 °F (15 °C) for thirty-six to forty-eight hours before adding to beer.

Gelatin

Because gelatin is a by-product of the degration/denaturation of isinglass, it is not used with cask-conditioned ales. Isinglass, on the other hand, tends to be expensive, particularly when in short supply.

Consequently, brewers who use collagen as a prefiltration aid have shown much more interest in gelatin as a fining agent. (For an historical summary, see Kindraka 1989.)

Gelatin is obtained from pork. After the pork skins are cleaned they go through an acid wash, after which collagen is extracted by additional processing. The finished product is sterile and ready for use at concentrations ranging from 60-90 milligrams per liter. Traditionally, gelatin is dissolved in water at 140-158 °F (60-70 °C) before addition, however, research suggests that 111 °F (44 °C) is adequate (Ibid.). Our test brews indicate that gelatin's yeast settling properties are around a factor of two to three under that obtained with the same concentration of isinglass.

Polyclar AT

Brewers of continental lagers do not use isinglass or gelatin since both involve processes that are not in compliance with Germany's Reinheitsgebot ("pledge of purity" law). In addition, a beer's foam stand tends to receive an elevated status on the Continent, as compared with the United Kingdom and the United States; therefore, fining agents that can potentially remove foam-positive proteins are not popular in Germany.

Alternatives are fining agents that work on the phenol side of the protein/phenol complex. The most popular of these is povidone (formerly known as polyvinylpyrrolidone), a powder derived from Nylon 66. The standard version is generally called Polyclar. Povidone is available in various grades of fineness. It works as an absorbent of tannins, with the finer grades having the greatest absorbency but requiring longer settling times.

The standard grade (Polyclar AT) is usually added at a rate of 30-50 grams per hectoliter of beer (Hums 1981), however, older versions of Nylon 66 required much higher concentrations (Coors 1977). The powder is diluted in de-aerated sterile water or sterile beer and added directly to beer in maturation tanks. Action is rapid, typically taking no longer than a few hours. In fact, new faster-acting versions have been proposed for use in conjunction with Kieselguhr in beer filtration (Maksuazawa and Nagashima 1990).

According to Hums (1981), at the 30-50 grams per hectoliter concentration, povidone absorbs 40-50% of haze-relevant tannins and 60-70% of anthocyanins. In test brews, we found this will result in Formazin Turbidity Units in the range of 125-175 for stressed beers. Moreover, beer foam is totally unaffected. At too high a dosage, povidone reduces color and affects hop bitterness; however, this requires concentrations near 1%, which is the same as 1,000 grams per hectoliter (twenty times what Hums suggests).

Povidone also removes virtually all oxidized polyphenols and melanoidins and, as a consequence, is sometimes cited as an antioxidant. This is somewhat deceptive, since in practical brewing by the time povidone is added, most of the oxidized phenols and melanoidins will have reacted with beer alcohols. This reaction results in the formation of various aldehydes, which are not removed by povidone. Nevertheless, this fining agent clearly deserves the widespread acceptance it has been accorded.

Silica Gel

Silica gel works on proteins through absorption and is noted for its efficiency in selecting haze-forming protein; when properly used, it will not remove foam-positive proteins. It was first introduced in Germany, although most development of its use was done in Europe and in the United States (Anger 1996; Feryhough and Ryder 1990). In recent years its acceptance among German brewers has increased dramatically (Maksuazawa et al. 1991), where it is seen as a natural companion to povidone. (Scheer provides an excellent overview of its use in U.S. microbreweries [Scheer 1990].)

In practical terms, silica gels are treated just like povidone. The concentration rate is the same, 30–50 grams per hectoliter, and it is added the same way as with povidone. Three versions of silica gel are available: (1) verogels, which are dusty like kieselguhr; (2) hydrogels, which have a 65% moisture content and are virtually dust free; and (3) gels of mineral origin, which tend to be less selective to haze proteins.

Enzymes

Various proteolytic enzymes stabilize beer by breaking down high molecular weight proteins into simpler structures (Woodward 1978). Papain is the most widely used. However, such products are relevant only to pasteurized beer, and even with pasteurized beer, contact times are brief (twenty-four to forty-eight hours). This is because the only practical way to denature proteolytic enzymes is with heat. These enzymes start with high molecular weight proteins, but in short order (days rather than weeks), they will destroy a beer's foam stand.

Beechwood Chips

The use of beechwood as a fining agent has a long and proud history in lager brewing. In many respects it is totally natural to the traditional lager process, when, near the end of the primary fermentation, the beer is transferred to closed vessels containing beechwood chips, and the fermentation is allowed to slowly go to completion. As this occurs, the yeast-laden chips fall from solution, thereby clarifying the beer. Our test brews indicate that this procedure is more efficient than one would think, although 30–50% less efficient than isinglass. Other studies show that the effect is purely geometrical. Thus, lightweight aluminum chips work just as well as beechwood and are easier to sanitize.

FILTRATION

Filtration, like fining, is a double-edged sword. If done right, it greatly enhances beer flavor by, among other things, removing dead yeast. It also plays a positive role in haze stability. On the downside, overfiltration emasculates beer, an effect that is obviously more important for bigger beer styles than for low-alcohol light beers.

Types of Filters

Filters fall into two categories: (1) deadhead filters, where beer flow is collinear with the flow of the filtrate; and (2) cross-flow filters, where the flow is at right angles (figure 5.1).

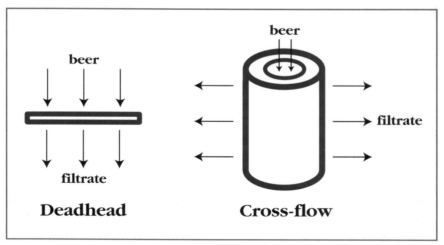

Figure 5.1. Types of filters.

The most common type of deadhead filter is the Kieselguhr leaf filter (Coors 1977). Kieselguhr comes from tiny algae that extract silicic acids from water to form their skeletons. The commercial brewing product is totally neutral to beer, and its use is permitted under the German purity law since it is considered a processing aid and not an ingredient. It is available in various grades, and grade choice depends on the thickness of filtration. Perlite, which is made of volcanic rock, is sometimes blended with Kieselguhr. Typical protocol for Kieselguhr filtration is as follows:

(1) In the first pre-coat, high-porosity Kieselguhr is mixed with beer at a dosage of 0.5–0.6 kilogram per square meter of the filter sheet area. As this mixture circulates through the filter, a coat forms on the filter sheets.
(2) In the second pre-coat, a grade of Kieselguhr of the same composition as the body feed is added at a dosage of 0.5–0.6 kilogram per square meter. This recirculates through the filter to form a second coat, as shown in figure 5.2.
(3) Once the pre-coats are established, recirculation is terminated and the filter goes on-line. During filtration, additional Kieselguhr is dosed in (called body feed). The total amount of Kieselguhr consumed is usually in the range of 120–160 grams per hectoliter.

Plate and frame filters are other deadhead filtration options. Whereas Kieselguhr filters require some practice to perfect their operation, plate and frame filters are completely user-friendly—one simply hooks them up and filtration begins. The downside is that plate and frame filters tend to be less flexible with respect to changes in the tightness of filtration than Kieselguhr filters. Perhaps the best-engineered version of a plate and frame system is the pulp filter used

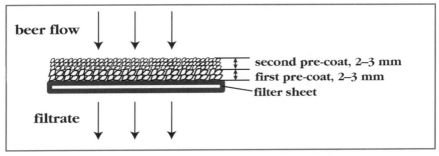

Figure 5.2. First and second pre-coats in Kieselguhr filtration process.

at the Coors Brewing Company in Boulder, Colorado (for a detailed discussion, see Beckett 1985).

Cross-flow filters with membranes are growing in popularity, and cartridge cross-flow filters have also attracted attention (Beer 1989; Ryder et al. 1988; Davis 1987; Gans et al. 1995; Wackerbauer 1992; Narziss, *Brauwelt* 1993, 5). A pilot version of a cartridge filter manufactured by Zahm and Nagel is shown in figure 5.3. These filters offer very precise control of filtration tightness. The major disadvantage with cross-flow filters is that they can plug, creating the need to back-flush through flow reversal at selected points.

A parameter of crucial importance is the micron rating of the filter, which, at the most basic level, is the diameter of the smallest particle that will be trapped on the filter. This is complicated by the influence of the operating conditions. For example, we have seen particulate of order 10 microns get jammed in filters rated at 0.5 μm by high-driving pressures. The one advantage of ceramic and stainless steel cartridges, like those shown in figure 5.3, is that excessive driving pressures will plug the filter and thus alert the operator that something is wrong. Back-flushing, by reversing the flow, typically unplugs the cartridge and filtration resumes. In contrast, high-driving pressures will cause cloth and vinyl cartridges to weaken, allowing large particles to pass. The same is true of Kieselguhr and plate and frame filters.

The Effects of Filtration
Table 5.4 lists the general effects of filtration at various micron levels. (See also Brantley and Aranha 1994.) Micron level refers to the actual micron rating, which may or may not be equal to the number quoted by manufacturers.

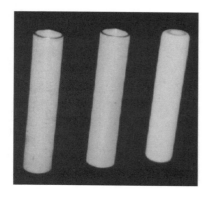

Figure 5.3. Cartridge filters.

An Analysis of Brewing Techniques

Table 5.4 Filtration Effectiveness

Micron Rating	Comments
6.00	This is a rough filtration, but it will clarify beer to some extent. Chill haze particles are not totally removed. Yeast biomass is usually reduced to below 1,000 cells per milliliter.
3.00	Similar, except that only young yeast cells penetrate. Mature and dead yeast are removed, and the total biomass is reduced to below 100 cells per milliliter. It offers a slightly better chill proofing than 6 microns.
1.00	Total yeast removal. Selected bacteria relevant to beer can penetrate, including *Lactobacilli* and *Pediococci*.
0.50	Total removal of bacteria known to be aggressive to beer. Selected bacteria of unknown relevance can penetrate.
0.22	Sterile filtration.

Table 5.5 Effects of Filtration

	Micron Rating	Apparent Extract (°P)	BU (mg/L)	Color (°L)	Cell Count (cells/mL)
Control (unfiltered beer)		2.50	27.5	4.6	10^5
	3.00	2.50	27.1	4.6	1–10
	1.00	2.45	26.2	3.9	0
	0.45	2.30	25.9	3.2	0

Based on these results, we feel the following are reasonable recommendations:

Filtration (microns)	Application
3–6	Draft beer served on-premise in brewpubs; in kegs from amateur brewers
3	Bottled beer locally distributed; standard homebrew
1	Bottled beer that may be stressed in trade
< 1	For bland beer only

Filtration can also influence the body and flavor of beer. Meier et al. (1995) found that a wide spectrum of particulates are trapped on membrane filters. The most common and the most responsible for beer filterability are beta-glucan/protein complexes. As the micron rating decreases, a broader spectrum of carbohydrates and proteins is removed. Table 5.5 summarizes our results using the Zahm and Nagel system and the three filters shown in figure 5.3. The strongest effects were the removal of carbohydrates and color. Some hop bitterness was removed, but the effect was weaker than anticipated. In a sense, this is bad news for submicron filtration, since it could totally disrupt the body and hop balance with the exception of lightly flavored beer with low hop flavors. Many megabrewers are filtering at the 0.45-0.5 μm level, and filtering at the 0.22 μm level has been proposed. It has been reported that such extreme filtration has no effect on beer flavor, however, these studies are confined to lighter beer styles (Burrel et al. 1994).

CARBONATION

Carbon Dioxide Units

In general, two units are used to express the carbon dioxide content of beer. In the Americas, it is expressed as a fraction based on the volume:

V = volumes of CO_2 = liters of CO_2 per liter of beer.

In Europe, it is expressed as a percentage on the basis of weight:

W = % CO_2 by weight = grams CO_2 per 100 grams of beer.

The density of carbon dioxide is approximately equal to 1.96 grams per liter. Hence, using the approximation that the density of water is 1,000 grams per liter (i.e., 1 kilogram per liter) we have

$V = SG \times W \times 10 / 1.96$

where SG is the specific gravity of the beer. For example, a carbon dioxide level by weight of 0.4 in a beer with a SG of 1.014 gives

$V = (1.014)(0.4)(10) / 1.96 = 2.07$ volumes.

A survey of carbon dioxide levels reported in the literature (Piendl 1970-1990) shows significant variation in the major beer styles. Some specific examples are cited in table 5.6.

An Analysis of Brewing Techniques

Table 5.6 Carbon Dioxide Levels in Beer

Brand	CO_2 Volumes
UK ales	
Bass (bottle)	2.27
Fullers ESB (bottle)	2.46
Whitbread (bottle)	2.31
German lagers	
König Pilsener	2.45
Veltin Pilsener	2.49
Salvator	2.28
Triumphator	2.63
US beer	
Coors	2.58
Budweiser	2.78
German wheat beer	
Weihenstephan Kristall Export	4.91
Späten Weisse	3.92
Löwen Weisse	4.15

Beer Foam

Recent research has distinguished beer constituents that are responsible for the formation of beer foam from those that contribute to foam's texture and retention (Heintz 1987; Siebert and Knudsen 1989; Melm, Tung, and Pringle 1995). In regard to its formation, dissolved carbon dioxide and moderate molecular weight proteins (molecular weights near 10,000 daltons) are most important. In striking contrast, foam stability is strongly enhanced by the presence of carbohydrate/protein complexes. The proteins consist of roughly 10% of the complex and have molecular weights around 40,000 daltons. This demonstrates how crucial malt types, malting procedures, and mashing procedures are to beer foam. Concerns regarding excess protein degradation were discussed previously, however, a beer's residual sugar content cannot be ignored either. Foam-negative constituents are listed in table 5.7.

Table 5.7 Foam-Negative Constituents

Constituent	Comments
Amino acids	Excessive degradation of wort proteins is doubly dangerous: (1) the amount of foam-positive protein is reduced; and (2) the amino acid pool (strongly foam negative) is increased. A balance is needed where the wort amino acid pool is sufficient for yeast metabolism but not much more than that.
Wort lipids	Lipids derived from wort trub play a role somewhat similar to that of amino acids. Yeast can use lipids advantageously in metabolism, however, any that spill over into finished beer will be foam negative. In addition, fatty acid fractions are easily oxidized, yielding staling off-flavors.
Lipids from yeast	In storage, residual yeast can sometimes excrete selected fatty acids, all of which are foam negative. Elevated storage temperatures encourage these effects.

Two other foam-negative factors, not listed in table 5.7 but just as important, are entirely preventable—dirty glassware and improper pouring. The harmful effects of residual grease and particulate matter on glassware are easy to demonstrate. We do not believe that the standard dishwasher soap used in homes and restaurants is adequate to clean beer glasses. Brushes, such as in the Spulboy system, are needed. Heavy grease (from lipstick, fatty foods, or fatty acid–based soaps) usually requires additional effort. The old brewer's trick of sprinkling sodium chloride (table salt) on glasses followed by a proper brush cleaning is remarkably effective.

The way beer is dispensed can also harm foam. Indeed, pouring beer from a bottle is erratic and done in any number of ways, which is why automated pouring devices are used in laboratory work. Nevertheless, we found a simple but reasonable way to check foam stability. Use an 8-ounce, clean brewery glass. With great care, pour the beer in such a way as to create 1 inch (2.5 centimeters) of foam. A good rule of thumb is that voids (thin surface layers where foam does not completely cover beer) should not appear in less than five minutes.

Direct Carbon Dioxide Injection

Directly injecting carbon dioxide into beer is the most widely used method, and in the absence of other considerations, the most recommended. If beer is to be transferred to a new tank, it is crucial to purge the receiving tank with carbon dioxide before transfer in order to reduce residual oxygen levels to as low as possible. The standard way to do this is to add carbon dioxide to the empty receiving tank, bringing the pressure to 10–15 psi. Within a few minutes the gases will stratify, with most of the lighter oxygen lying above the carbon dioxide. Venting the tank just before transfer will result in a purge of most of the oxygen. Transferring beer via carbon dioxide pressure, and at the same time allowing a slight gas bleed from the receiving tank, will virtually remove all oxygen.

Once the receiving tank is filled, one of three processes can be used:

- Autocarbonation
- Feed and rock system
- Feed and bleed system

To illustrate these ideas, suppose a carbon dioxide content of 2.5 volumes is desired. Since the absorption of carbon dioxide increases with decreasing temperature, beer carbonation is usually done as close to 32 °F (0 °C) as possible. Suppose for the purpose of illustration, carbonation takes place at 35 °F (2 °C). In appendix E, table E.1 shows that at equilibrium this is equal to a pressure of 10 psi. The trick is to achieve equilibrium conditions.

With autocarbonation, one simply injects the required amount of carbon dioxide into the tank. In our example, this amounts to 2.5 liters of carbon dioxide per liter of beer, which is the same as 2.5 hectoliters per hectoliter of beer. Eventually, the carbon dioxide is absorbed into the beer. We found this procedure to be highly erratic, and it is not recommended for general use.

The feed and rock system is sometimes used in amateur brewing to speed up the process. In this system, the tank is filled with the appropriate amount of carbon dioxide then rocked vigorously to force the system into equilibrium. This method works in the sense that equilibrium can be reached in minutes rather than days or weeks, as in the case with autocarbonation. The feed and rock system's weak point is the possibility of residual air in the carbonation tank, which would then carbonate and oxidate beer simultaneously.

The feed and bleed system is an attractive alternative. Assuming a temperature of 35 °F (2 °C), 2.5 volumes of carbon dioxide is dissolved by feeding the carbon dioxide into the tank at 10–12 psi. At the same time, a slight amount of gas is allowed to bleed from the tank, thereby stripping any residual oxygen from both the beer and the carbonation tank. The time required to reach equilibrium with the feed and bleed system is greatly reduced by the system's carbonating stone, which breaks carbon dioxide into tiny bubbles that are readily absorbed. The classic Zahm and Nagel feed and bleed system is shown in figure 5.4. It is a 50-liter version of systems used in commercial brewing. The ceramic carbonating stone is rated at 0.5 μm and is attached to the gas line.

Figure 5.4. Classic Zahm and Nagel feed and bleed system.

The following procedure provides good results: (1) Pack the carbonation tank in some ice to keep the temperature in the range of 34–35 °F (1–2 °C). (2) In a warm environment (say in excess of 68 °F [20 °C]), add salt to the ice. (3) Inject carbon dioxide with the feed and bleed system in one- or two-minute feeding sessions, which are repeated every ten minutes. Equilibrium is usually achieved within an hour. (4) After finishing the feeding sessions, let the beer rest for about thirty minutes before bottling.

Kraeusening
The traditional method for carbonating lagers is to transfer them to closed tanks that have 0.5–1% fermentable sugar remaining. A slow secondary fermentation allows a buildup of carbon dioxide to the 2.8–3.0 volume range. Excess is bled off to get the desired pre-filled carbon dioxide content. This method is tricky and subject to error

and often leads to corrections with a kraeusen (i.e., bulk carbonation with fresh wort and yeast). When kraeusening was first introduced, it was viewed with some contempt, since it was used only to correct errors in the traditional process. However, as our understanding of fermentation increased, particularly with respect to the formation and reduction of by-products, a preference developed for allowing the fermentation to go to completion before transfer. In this circumstance, kraeusening during maturation became a necessity, and respect for the procedure increased accordingly.

Kraeusening has been characterized as a method of "natural carbonation" to distinguish it from direct carbon dioxide injection, which gets labeled "artificial carbonation." These labels imply that natural carbonation yields better beer foam. We use both on a regular basis and find no evidence to suggest one gives better beer foam than the other. Furthermore, the issues discussed at the beginning of the chapter regarding foam are vastly more important than the method of carbonation used.

Kraeusen is useful in dealing with unexpected high diacetyl levels at the fermentation end point. In particular, if the latter is at 0.25 milligram per liter or higher, our experience shows that even lengthy maturation periods will not reduce it below the standard target of 0.1 milligram per liter. However, if the beer is kraeusened with fresh yeast of high viability, the mistakes made by the yeast used in the original fermentation can be corrected. Indeed, we have seen diacetyl levels drop from the 0.25–0.35 milligram per liter range to below 0.05 milligram per liter after kraeusening. On the other hand, kraeusening with dysfunctional yeast can have the opposite effect.

We find it useful to kraeusen with a volume equal to 15–20% of the volume of beer to be carbonated. A cold tolerant yeast strain, such as W-34/70, is preferred, at a second fermentation temperature range of 41–45 °F (5–7 °C). It is advisable to start the priming solution in a separate tank and to pitch it when it reaches high kraeusen. This creates slightly more carbon dioxide than needed, so venting the kraeusen tank is necessary; therefore, as with direct injection, instrumentation to monitor pressure is required.

Bottle Refermentation

Adding yeast and either sugar or wort to bottles to condition beer has been done for centuries. Such a procedure gives the finished beer special flavors that are not present if the beer is simply carbonated, either by direct injection or with a kraeusen. Bottle refermentation gains flavor only with certain beer styles, such as German wheat beers, where bottle refermentation is seen as crucial to the hefeweizen style (Warner 1992). The same is true of select and highly praised English and Belgian ales.

Several studies have been conducted that investigated the special characteristics of bottle refermentation (Derdelinckx et al. 1992; Warner 1992). In the first study, it was found that the fermentation displayed strong abnormalities with respect to respiration. This in turn led to elevated levels of isoamyl acetate (banana flavor), and, in various bottle-conditioned Belgian ales, to elevated levels of ethyl caproate (apple flavor). Consistent with this was the finding that only 30% of the air in the bottle's headspace was consumed during the bottle refermentation, and the remaining 70% was ultimately absorbed into the beer. Tests were done to see if adding oxygen at filling would induce something closer to a normal respiratory cycle, and it was found that this only hastened the onset of staling (Derdelinckx et al. 1992). In addition, all of the effects were present regardless of how the beer was primed (i.e., with sugar or with wort).

The above results are consistent with folklore associated with bottle refermentation. For example, in Germany it has long been felt that bottle conditioning plays a special role in developing a weizen's soft and attractive clove/banana finish. Not only does the research cited previously confirm this, but attempts to mimic the authentic flavor profile, using estery yeast in the primary fermentation and forced carbonation, have dismally failed. The special fruitiness found in select Belgian ales also would not be possible without bottle conditioning. However, the research clearly shows why bottle conditioning has not found favor with all beer styles.

Carbon dioxide levels in bottle-conditioned beer vary widely, and in general, they tend to be high. This is not only the case with wheat beers, it applies to other ale styles as well; therefore, the amount of priming solution added is crucial. The classic rule for brewers' sugar (which is 100% fermentable) is

$$A = 2B - 0.3 \times C - R$$

where A is the concentration of prime in grams per liter, B is the desired carbon dioxide level in grams per liter, and C is the concentration of residual fermentable sugars. The factor 0.3 is used to account for maltotriose, which is usually 70% of the residual and is not metabolized in bottle refermentation. R is the carbon dioxide residual in grams per liter (Ibid.).

For example, suppose that a fully attenuated beer (C equals 0) is to be carbonated to three volumes (i.e., 3 liters of carbon dioxide per liter of beer). Using a carbon dioxide density of 2 grams per liter, the desired carbon dioxide level is

B = 2 x 3 = 6 grams per liter.

If stored beer is kept under a modest carbon dioxide cover, say 5-7.5 psi at 35 °F (2 °C), the residual carbon dioxide in the beer will rarely be above one volume. Using this figure we get

R = 2 x 1 = 2 grams per liter;

thus, the amount of sugar to add is

A = 2 x 6 - 2 = 10 grams per liter.

New yeast is often pitched when priming for bottle refermentation. Warner (1992) quotes repitching rates for German wheat beers in the range of 2-4 milliliters yeast per liter. With Belgian and English ales, much less yeast is used, typically at a factor twenty below the values given by Warner (Derdelinckx et al. 1992). In both cases, filling is generally done at 72 °F (22 °C), and conditioning is allowed to proceed at temperatures as high as 75 °F (24 °C).

BOTTLING BEER

We have long felt that there is something fundamentally unnatural about transferring beer into tiny 10–12-ounce bottles. Practical considerations force us to use such packaging, however the process is not a pleasant one and requires a mind-set of damage control. Two major problem areas are: (1) air ingress into the bottle during the fill; and (2) ingress of bacteria, molds, and yeast into the bottle.

Bottle fillers vary significantly in price and complexity, but they all are based on the following principles:

Pre-evacuation: A vacuum is inserted into the bottle and draws out the oxygen.

Counterpressure: Carbon dioxide injection into the bottle immediately following pre-evacuation.

Counterpressure fill: Beer is pushed into the bottle at a slightly higher pressure than the counterpressure, resulting in a laminar flow.

Foaming: A final oxygen-reduction measure to induce foaming when the bottle is filled. Ideally, the bottle is capped when the foam reaches the top of the bottle.

Modern bottle fillers fully optimize all four stages. When operated properly, air levels below 0.15 milliliter per 12-ounce bottle can be obtained. Older bottle fillers and amateur counterpressure fillers (see figure 5.5) generally are not equipped with the pre-evacuation option. Nevertheless, it has been our experience that air levels as low as 0.50 milliliter per bottle can still be achieved, however proper foaming is crucial in such cases. The goal is for the foam at the end of the fill to displace as much air as possible without the beer overflowing.

Operator error can be significant with counterpressure fillers. For example, the air levels reported in a comparative study of counterpressure fillers were around a factor of 5–10 higher than what could have been achieved under optimized conditions (Ruggiero, Spillane, and Snyder 1995). This is not unusual, and even highly skilled brewers typically need practice with unfamiliar counterpressure fillers to obtain optimal air and finished beer carbon dioxide levels.

Figure 5.5. An amateur counterpressure filler.

Recent research on the flavor stability of bottled beer shows that it is indeed important to keep bottle air levels low. However, a more significant factor is the way beer is stored. In particular, thermal abuse can greatly hasten the onset of staling. This is shown in figure 5.6. Consider the case of beer which has 2.0 milliliters of air (per one-third liter of beer). This was typical of the high air levels reported in Ruggiero et. al (1995). If this beer is stored at 42 °F (6 °C), then staling should not be evident until at least eighty days. However, at 86 °F (30 °C) it will be

An Analysis of Brewing Techniques

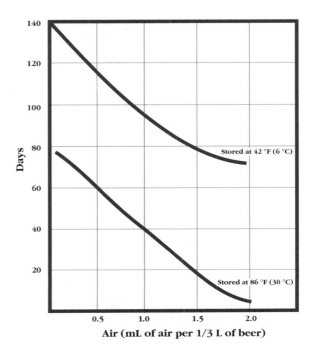

Figure 5.6.
The formation of stale flavors during storage.

Stored at 42 °F (6 °C)

Stored at 86 °F (30 °C)

Days

Air (mL of air per 1/3 L of beer)

apparent within a week or so. To cite one more example, consider the case of beer which has 0.1 milliliter of air. This is the level achieved in modern commercial fillers. When stored at 42 °F (6 °C), it will have a shelf life of four months or more. However, storage at 86 °F (30 °C) will give a shelf life of only eighty days, almost the same as the beer with 2.0 milliliters of air that was not thermally abused (i.e., stored at 42 °F [6 °C]).

Wine and spirits are not as sensitive to thermal stress as beer (Amerine, Berg, and Cruess 1972); as a consequence, many distributors are not aware that beer requires special handling. This is particularly true for the more flavorful beers. In fact, this is an area where "the bigger the beer, the harder it falls." Our concern is that the increase in stale beer due to thermal stress will suppress the beer movement more than all the prohibitionists combined could.

Beer is a rather hostile environment for microbial activity. The presence of alcohol and low pH are important factors, as is the absence of elementary carbohydrates in fully attenuated brews. On the other hand, compounds produced by microbes in bottled beer can have very low thresholds (for example, see Anderson et al. 1995). Because of mold contamination in the fill area, musty (also earthy, woody) effects occasionally appear in beer. One of the responsible compounds, trichloroanisole, was shown to be detectable in concentrations as low as four parts per trillion!

Offending microbes are airborne and gain entry into bottles via dust particles (Ibid.; Christiansen 1995). Thus, not only is it important to rigorously clean and sanitize filling equipment, but the fill working area must receive the same treatment as well. Modern breweries have "clean rooms" where bottles are filled in an essentially sterile environment. In the absence of this, the following measures are useful:

(1) Mop the fill area with a quaternary ammonium compound. Be sure to also rigorously treat corners and walls near the fillers.
(2) Minimize downtimes; studies show that contamination primarily occurs during start ups. Ideally, the fill should be uninterrupted.
(3) Have a 70% ethanol solution on hand in a spray bottle. Spray anything that touches beer at the start of the fill and every fifteen minutes thereafter (a large brewery has found success with peracetic acid). Non-neutral sanitizers, such as chlorine, should not be used.
(4) Conduct a microbiological analysis of samples on a regular basis (see Microbiological Analysis in chapter 6).

An Analysis of Brewing Techniques

6

Evaluation of Beer

BASIC DATA

Maintaining a record of numerical data associated with each brew is a useful part of quality assurance and control. This data can include:

- Original extract
- Brew house yield
- Forced fermentation data: real extract, real degree of fermentation, apparent extract, and apparent degree of fermentation
- Main fermentation data: real extract, real degree of fermentation, apparent extract, and apparent degree of fermentation
- Bittering units (BU)
- pH: mash, wort, fermented wort, and beer
- Carbon dioxide volumes
- Air .
- Percent alcohol by weight
- Caloric content
- Flavor problems
- Color

The percent alcohol by weight and caloric value of a beer can be measured or computed with the following:

$$A = (OE - AE) / (2.0665 - 0.010665 \times OE)$$

and

$$C = [6.9 \times A + 4 \times (RE - 0.1)] \times 3.55 \times SG$$

where *A* is percent alcohol by weight, *OE* is the original extract, *AE* is apparent extract, *C* is caloric value, *RE* is real extract, and *SG* is the specific gravity of the beer. We found both formulas to be remarkably accurate, with errors less than 1% over the extract range of 0–30 °P.

When flavor problems appear, additional data typically are needed to identify the source of the problem. Of particular interest are the levels of important fermentation by-products (see Fermentation By-products in chapter 3) including:

- Diacetyl
- Esters: ethyl acetate and amyl acetate
- Fusel alcohols: amyl alcohol and phenyl ethanol
- Acetaldehyde
- Sulfur compounds

Flavor analysis can be done by consultants, a consulting laboratory, or in-house using the protocols given in *ASBC Methods of Analysis* (1992).

Color is another useful variable to monitor. There has always been a strong preference for visual units to be used for evaluating and determining beer color. There are many reasons for this, not the least of which is that classic beer styles are defined in part by definite visual images of what is appropriate. In this book, we adopted the Lovibond 52 scale because of its wide use in the Americas. In Europe, conceptually similar units are used. Unfortunately, there is not an accurate way to translate between the two systems, except with light-colored beers (Fix, *Zymurgy* 1988). Thus, we found it necessary to use one scale or the other and to use the same units for all color-related issues. Table 6.1 provides examples using the Lovibond 52 scale.

In other applications, color is defined in different ways. For example, spectrophotometric measurements at wavelengths relevant to the application are often used. In the 1950s, it was discovered that pale beer absorbance measured in this way was essentially proportional to visual units like the Lovibond scale. In 1958, the American Society of Brewing Chemists (ASBC) proposed a standard measure be used for beer absorbance; namely, in a 1/2-inch internal diameter (ID) jar using a monochromatic light with a wavelength of 430 nanometers. They proposed a correction factor of ten so the numbers (called degrees SRM) reported would match up with the Lovibond scale.

An Analysis of Brewing Techniques

Table 6.1 Lovibond 52 Scale Beer Examples

Color	Hue	°L Range	Beer (°L)
Yellow	Light	2.0–3.0	Budweiser (2.0)
	Medium	3.0–4.5	König Pilsner (3.1)
			Dortmunder Actien-Export (3.8)
			Pilsner Urquell (4.2)
	Deep straw/gold	4.5–6.0	Späten Club Weisse (4.6)
			Kuppers Kölsch (4.8)
	Deep gold	6.0–7.5	Giesler Kölsch (6.5)
Amber	Light	7.5–9.0	Pinkus Münstersch Alt (7.5)
	Full	9.0–11.0	Bass Pale Ale (10)
			Whitbread Pale Ale (11)
	Red/brown	11–14	Düssel-Alt (12.5)
	Brown	14–17	Michelob Dark (17)
Black	Brown/black	17–20	Rheinisch Alt (18)
	Medium black	20–25	Salvator (21)
			Sud-Alt (23)
	Start of full black	> 25	Triumphator (27)

Commercial beer brewed at this time was almost always below 4 °L, so SRM became viewed as an equivalent of °L. Nevertheless, as beer color moves into the amber range, the relationship between visual and spectrophotometric units starts to diverge sharply. The primary reason for this is that the human eye detects a wide spectrum of wavelengths from a color source, whereas spectrophotometers work only at selected wavelengths. The spectrophotometric units have the advantage that absorbency relationships such as Beer's law are valid, whereas this law fails measurably in visual units like the Lovibond scale. On the other hand, for amber beers the spectrophotometric units are devoid of visual interpretation. Indeed, there are examples of beers which have dramatically different visual colors yet also have the same absorbency at 430 nanometers.

Large commercial breweries continue to use spectrophotometry, even with the amber and dark beers they have recently started brewing. Their approach has typically been to develop new in-house correction factors for each of their brews that allow them to match up absorbance with the Lovibond scale within the range of variations seen in production. We prefer the dilution method (see Fix, *Zymurgy* 1988) in lab work where accurate color measurements are needed.

When protocol is carefully followed, errors using this procedure are less than 1%. For normal color determination, such as when designing a recipe or judging a competition, the Davison color chart has proven to be satisfactory (Davison 1993). If it is properly used, errors will be 5% or less.

Even visual units start to become highly suspect once the full black regime is reached. For example, we have seen highly qualified national judges incorrectly distinguish beers at 40, 50, and 60 °L. This is the primary reason the dilution procedure just mentioned starts at 17 °L. In the past, experts suggested diluting samples with water before determining color (*ASBC Methods of Analysis* 1958). Given the inherent nonlinearities, this would require correction factors be used in order to obtain consistent results. On the other hand, a strong case can be made that once a beer is in the full black regime, flavor-oriented issues should dominate the evaluation—color considerations at this point "pale" in comparison!

MICROBIOLOGICAL ANALYSIS

The microbiological analysis of beer is significantly more complicated than that for yeast, primarily because the maximum acceptable microbial level is much less for packaged beer than it is for yeast. In large industrial brewing, the criterion of not more than one microbial cell per 100 milliliters is widely used for unpasteurized bottled beer. In practical terms, this is close to complete sterility. There were two highly publicized product recalls by megabrewers in the 1990s that were an indication that this criterion is by no means frivolous; rather, it is necessary for unpasteurized bottled beer that is subject to market abuse.

Less stringent criteria can be used for draft beer, homebrew, and beer served at brewpubs. Our experience is that the criterion used at the Siebel Institute of Technology in Chicago, Illinois, of no more than one cell per milliliter, is a good working rule. The only possible exception is homebrew that is shipped to a distant location for a competition under unfavorable conditions.

It has been our experience that elementary media, like HLP, are hopelessly inadequate to detect bacteria at the levels previously cited. Much greater resolution is required. Brewers with well-equipped labs are showing a growing preference for Nachweismedium für Bierschadliche Bacterium. This sophisticated medium is highly accurate (it can detect microbes at the one cell per 100 milli-liter level), fast (results in five to six days), and natural (composed of 50% beer). The downside of this medium is that it is extremely user-unfriendly, and control over pH and other parameters is well beyond the capabilities of most small breweries.

The following procedure is an effective alternative to sophisti-cated media. It is natural (25% beer), accurate, and user-friendly. While it takes longer to get results, this is not a serious problem, as long as the procedure is used as a routine quality-assurance tool to detect problems rather than as part of crisis management. The fol-lowing are needed:

(1) Universal brewer's agar is available at scientific outlets (see table 6.2 for a list of ingredients). (Prepare petri dishes containing the medium with the procedures described in the Slant Preparation section of chapter 2.) Add Acti-Dione to the 30 milligrams per liter to half of the plates (i.e., petri dishes); the other half should have no inhibitors.

(2) A brewers' jar, such as shown in figure 6.1, to use as an anaero-bic chamber. Half the plates will be kept in anaerobic conditions. Special chambers are available for this, but they tend to be expensive and, in our opinion, unnecessary. Most of the anaero-bic bacteria relevant to beer (e.g., strains of *Lactobacillus*, *Pediococcus*, *Pectinatus*, and *Megasphaera*) are not pure anaer-obes, and the presence of oxygen at sufficiently low levels will

Figure 6.1. A brewer's jar.

not be inhibitory. Place the plates and a lit candle inside the jar. By the time the candle burns out, only subliminal amounts of oxygen will remain.

Procedure

(1) Test the brewer's jar. It is important to periodically check the brewer's jar. We use a Universal Brewer's Agar plate with a strong anaerobe (our favorite is *Lactobacillus pastorianus*) inoculated at the ten to fifteen cells per milliliter level. Hold the temperature at 77 °F (25 °C), then growth can usually be seen within ninety-six hours. At 68 °F (20 °C), a couple more days may be needed. No growth indicates that the arrangement is not effectively excluding oxygen.

(2) Three sample beers are needed for this procedure. All should be stored in a water bath at 86 °F (30 °C).

(3) At the end of a week, chill one of the stressed beers to 50 °F (10 °C) and taste it against an unstressed sample. Generally, this will give an overall impression of the microbiological state of the beer.

(4) At the end of the second week, inoculate four plates; two with Acti-Done and two without. The best way to inoculate is to pour beer over a 0.21 µm filter and transfer the material trapped on the filter to the plate. Do this inside a transfer box to prevent picking up ambient microbes.

(5) Leave two aerobic plates (one with Acti-Done and one without) in a clean open area at 77–86 °F (25–30 °C); place the other two anaerobic plates inside the brewer's jar at the same temperature.

(6) No growth after seven days is typically equivalent to cell counts below one per 10 milliliters. Microscopy can be used to analyze growth.

EVALUATING FLAVOR

Beer evaluation has conceptual, physiological, and psychological components. All are discussed in this section.

The Meilgaard System of Categorization

The diversity that exists in beer is staggering; therefore, before any serious evaluation can be done, a clear and unambiguous description of the desired beer profile must be developed. In the past, conceptual descriptions were hampered by the frequent use of vague and ill-defined descriptors that generally meant different things to different people.

Dr. Morton Meilgaard made a major advance when he led a team of flavor chemists in a project that identified and analyzed all of the flavor-relevant compounds in beer (Meilgaard 1991). The flavor wheel, a product of this research, is now the internationally accepted thesaurus for beer flavor descriptors—both taste and smell.

The flavor wheel is actually a collection of eight trees (using graph theory). The highest level in each of the eight classes represents the broadest description of the perceived flavors. Within each of these are level 1 subcategories that add definition to the description; within each level 1 subcategory are level 2 subcategories that further define a flavor.

The first of the eight classes—Category 1000—is the most basic in that it employs everyday terminology, that even people without any specialized knowledge of beer or brewing can understand and use to evaluate beer (figure 6.2).

Table 6.2 Composition of Universal Brewer's Agar

Component	Weight
Tomato juice broth	25.0 g
Peptonized milk	15.0 g
Dextrose	10.0 g
Agar	12.0 g
Distilled water	750.0 mL
Beer	250.0 mL

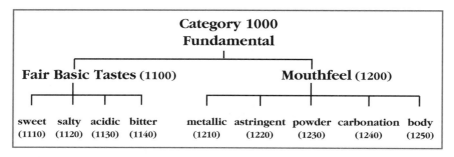

Figure 6.2. Category 1000 is the fundamental class of the flavor wheel.

The next seven classes (figures 6.3–6.6) make varying degrees of technical demands on the taster, and the untutored may feel uncomfortable using them. However, the first of these, Category 2000, is important in the sense that it is relevant to all known beer styles.

It is also the classification where complex and sophisticated beers are distinguished from less-inspiring versions.

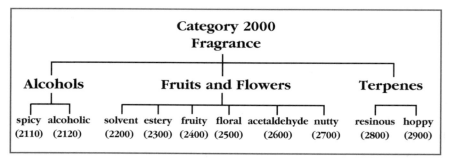

Figure 6.3. This fragrance class is relevant to all known beer styles.

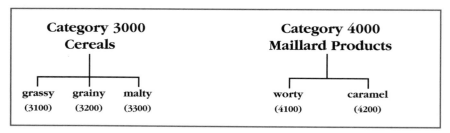

Figure 6.4. Category 3000 deals with properties related to grains, and the 4000 class concerns heterocyclics associated with wort production.

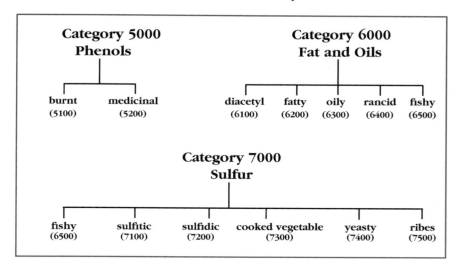

Figure 6.5. Categories 5000, 6000, and 7000 have to do with defects resulting from technical errors in brewing.

An Analysis of Brewing Techniques

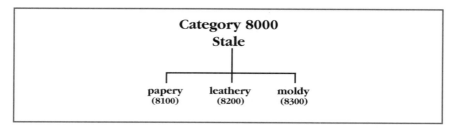

Figure 6.6. Category 8000 represents flavor tones that ultimately appear in all beer, no matter how well made. Brewers should work hard to delay staling.

An intensity bar chart is another tool that helps us conceptualize a beer profile. It is a graphical representation of the flavor wheel that records the desired intensities of individual flavor tones. We prefer the five-point DLG system, which uses the following grade system to rate intensity levels:

1 = not detectable
2 = slightly detectable
3 = detectable but not strong
4 = strong
5 = overpowering

To illustrate, the bar chart in figure 6.7 represents the ideal profile of an English-style extra special bitter. The shaded areas represent the desired intensity ranges. English-style extra special bitters are complex beers. The bar charts for such beers typically have many peaks, with several intensity grades in the 2.5–3.5 range and a few in the 3.5–4 range. Bland beers have no peaks above 2.5, while one-dimensional beers have only one peak above 3.5–4 and no others. For example, some inferior India pale ale formulations have only one spike—4 or higher—in the hoppy category.

English-style extra special bitters have above average original gravities (typically 1.048–1.060; 12–15 °P); therefore the alcohol in these beers is detectable but not overpowering. Inferior versions of the style are often underattenuated, which leads to worty, unfermented tones that are a serious defect. The complexity of this ale comes from its estery/fruity tones that should be detectable but not overpowering. Because this ale is made with English hops, it is not as floral as U.S. pale ales, although that tone is not totally absent.

Ironically, English-style extra special bitters made with significant amounts of East Kent Goldings hops tend to have grassy tones, although this flavor constituent is in the cereal category of the Meilgaard system. The color malts used to produce these rather rich malty beers also leave detectable caramel tones. There may be some diacetyl present, but any hint of sulfur is a major defect.

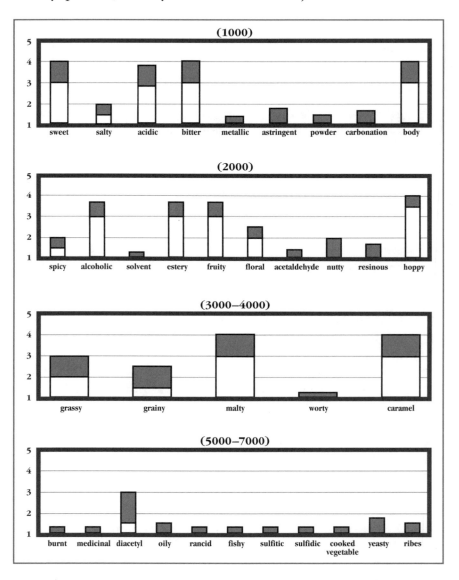

Figure 6.7. Intensity levels of an ideal English-style extra special bitter beer.

An Analysis of Brewing Techniques

Category 8000 is not represented in figure 6.7 because the flavor tones in this category should not be present in this beer style. Bar charts of actual English-style extra special bitters, particularly imported commercial versions available in the United States, often have some 8000 category flavors present. If those flavors approach the 2.5–3.0 intensity level, the entire bar chart will dramatically change shape and

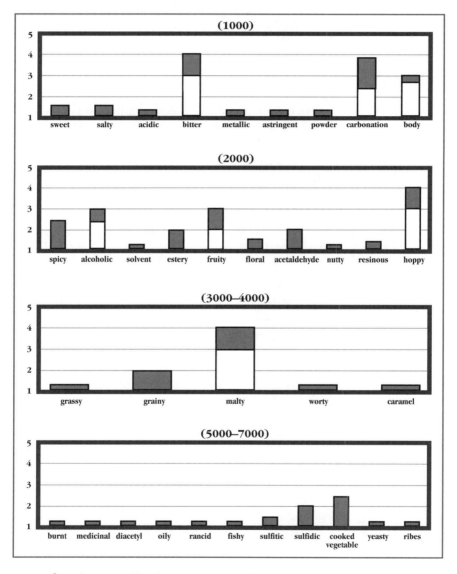

Figure 6.8. Flavor profile of a continental-style Pilsener.

depart rather significantly from the ideal. In extreme cases, rancid tones can reach the 4-5 intensity level and dominate the entire beer flavor. Attempting to profile such a beer can be an uninspiring enterprise.

Let's also consider a continental-style Pilsener (figure 6.8). The original gravity of these beers is slightly below that of English-style extra special bitters (11–13 °P; 1.044–1.052), therefore the alcohol bar is lower. Many style descriptions assert that estery and/or fruity tones should not be detectable, but this is nonsense. As noted in chapter 3, these are common flavor elements of all existing beer styles (selected nonalcohol beers are the exception). It is true, however, that in Pilseners the estery/fruity tones are quite delicate and subtle. In most well-made Pilseners, the bulk of the perceived fruitiness comes from hops. The same can be said for spicy tones, which invariably are present when high farnesene "noble-type" hops (e.g., Saaz and Tettnanger) are used. Although all of these tones are subtle, they greatly enhance the complexity of Pilsener beer.

The heart of Pilseners, as for all continental-style lagers, is the special malty/sulphury complex of flavor tones that stem from the finest Pilsener malt and select yeast strains like W-34/70 and W-206. These tones, which should be very rounded and free of harshness, are sometimes difficult to categorize within Meilgaard's system. Sulphur tones have some aspect of dimethyl sulfate and usually hint of sweet corn (some use the unflattering term "onion effect"). Pilseners are also very clean beers. Flavor tones from either the 5000 or 6000 category have typically negative effects. In our opinion, diacetyl is as damaging to lagers as sulphur flavors are to ales.

Physiological and Psychological Components

The so-called "human factor" in beer evaluation relates to the ability to correctly detect and identify the flavor tones present and to accurately characterize their intensity levels. Errors can come from any of the following:

- Temporary palate bias
- Permanent palate bias
- Physiological factors
- Psychological factors

Temporary palate bias is the easiest to describe and detect. Colds, congestion, temporary respiratory problems, and overconsumption of food and/or drink can cause palate dullness. Effects of the latter can last twenty-four hours or longer. The most effective way to detect palate dullness is with the triangle test. Present two beers of similar composition and character to the person being tested. Use three identical glasses, two of which contain the same beer. The person tries to determine the odd beer by tasting and smelling all three beer samples. This test is frequently administered to members of professional flavor panels. If a panel member fails the test he or she is removed from the panel for that particular tasting session.

Just as there are some people who are colorblind, there are those who are blind to certain flavors; and just as there are natural-born athletes, there are people whose palates have always been sensitive and highly accurate. At the same time, there are self-made athletes, people who are not endowed with inborn skills but who succeed by "playing smart." Analogously, there are people who have become skilled beer evaluators, not because of an innate gift, but through education and experience. They "taste smart" in that they are aware of flavors they are overly sensitive to as well as flavors that are difficult for them to detect. In any given situation they are able to think and taste their way through an evaluation, accurately identifying the flavor tones present at the correct intensity levels. Professional panelists are monitored on a regular basis by comparing their profiles of standard beers with consensus profiles.

Table 6.3
Bias in Beer Evaluation—Meilgaard's Physiological Factors

Factor	Example
Adaptation	After having tasted a set of bitter beers, the subject is unable to accurately score a less bitter sample.
Cross-adaptation	The subject is insensitive to the sweetness in beer because of the sweetness of previous samples.
Potentiation	The subject perceives more bitterness in a bitter beer because the sample followed a set of sweet beers.
Enhancement	The presence of amyl alcohols enhances the rose flavor of phenylethanyl.
Synergy	Fruity tones, from selected esters with fruity tones and from selected hop varieties, can yield a fruity tone that is stronger than the sum of individual intensities. (Note: Meilgaard does not regard this effect to be relevant to beer.)
Suppression/masking	A high level of hop bitterness and aroma can mask the presence of diacetyl.

(Adapted from Meilgaard, Dalgliesh, and Clapperton 1979 with permission of the publisher.)

Research shows that physiological and psychological factors are major sources of error in beer evaluation. Meilgaard and his colleagues studied these issues extensively; and the material in tables 6.3–6.5 is taken (with minor modifications) from their work (Meilgaard, Dalgliesh, and Clapperton 1979). The effects of presentation order are displayed separately (table 6.5) because of their relevance to beer competitions. In Meilgaard's work, they are included in table 6.4.

Table 6.4
Bias in Beer Evaluation—Meilgaard's Psychological Factors

Factor	Example
Expectation error	The subject is given information about a sample before it is tasted.
Error of habituation	A tendency to give the same response when samples show low levels of variation.
Stimulus error	The subject is influenced by a beer's container or label.
Logical error	A very dark bock beer may be rated as more favorable. Another example occurs when a Pilsener that is slightly darker than normal may be rated as more stale than it actually is.
Halo effect	A positive (negative) reaction to one attribute causes the overevaluation (underevaluation) of other attributes.
Mutual suggestion	A panel member loudly says, "Eeech."
Lack of motivation	A disinterested panelist.
Capriciousness vs. timidity	The capricious panelist gives extreme intensity ratings that exert too much influence on a panel's results, while the timid panelist sticks to a narrow band in the center of the scale, exerting too little influence.

(Adapted from Meilgaard, Dalgliesh, and Clapperton 1979 with permission of the publisher.)

Table 6.5 Bias in Beer Evaluation—Effects of Presentation Order

Factor	Example
Positional bias due to time	In short tests, the first sample usually rates highest (due to anticipation or thirst); in long tests, the last tends to be rated highest.
Positional bias due to central tendency	The three middle samples in a set of five samples tend to be rated higher in hop aroma and lower in oxidation flavor.
Pattern effect	If flavorable samples are consistently served late in tests, panelists often give higher flavor intensity ratings to samples presented late.
Contrast effect	A bland sample presented immediately after a flavorful one might be rated as blander than it actually is.
Group effect	A bland sample in the midst of many flavorful ones might be rated as more flavorable than it actually is.

(Adapted from Meilgaard, Dalgliesh, and Clapperton 1979 with permission of the publisher.)

An Analysis of Brewing Techniques

IMPROVING COMPETITIVE JUDGING

We decided to end this chapter by sharing our views on improving beer judging in competitions. We propose that an *anonymous* evaluation of judges take place in concurrence with the *anonymous* evaluation of each particular beer style. Each judge's evaluation score will then determine the weight of his or her score in the final beer score. For each beer category, we suggest the following procedure:

(1) Select two ringers for the beer category—fresh, mainstream representatives of the style. A consensus score (determined by the competition's organizers) is established for each ringer, plus an acceptable deviation (e.g., 40 plus or minus 1).
(2) The triangle test is administered to each member of the panel.
(3) The ringers are introduced into the evaluation (e.g., one early, one late) as if they are regular entries.

Each judge starts with a score of one. As there are three possible errors, each error reduces his or her score by one third. Errors include (1) failing the triangle test, (2) giving the first ringer a score outside the target range, and (3) giving the second ringer a score outside the target range. The final score for a regular entry in a beer category is the weighted average of the judges' scores for that entry.

The example in figure 6.9 was taken from a test given at a sanctioned competition. We consider it to be representative of the improvements a weighted evaluation system would make over the current system.

Figure 6.9. Category—Continental Pilsener

Ringer 1—Warsteiner: target score = 36 (±1)

Ringer 2—König Pilsner: target score = 40 (±1)

Beer—Homebrewed Pilsener, tasted second among 12 beers

Judge	Triangle Test	Score Ringer 1	Score Ringer 2	Score Beer	Weight	Weighted Score
1	pass	37	41	38	1	38.0
2	pass	35	38	37	2/3	24.8
3	fail	36	35	34	1/3	11.3
4	fail	36	32	26	0	0.0
			Total =	135	2	74.1
			Avg. = 135 / 4 = 33.75			74.1 / 2 = 37.1

Using the current system, the judges' average score for the second beer tasted was 33.75; the weighted-system score was 37. In a competitive category, such as continental-style Pilseners, a weighted system could significantly change the rankings. (Note that the fourth judge was either having a bad day or simply did not understand the category!)

An Analysis of Brewing Techniques

Basic Units

Prefixes for metric units:

kilo 1,000	deci 0.1
hecto 100	centi 0.01
deka 10	milli 0.001

Metric and U.S. volumetric units and abbreviations:

hectoliter (hL)	barrel (bbl.)
liter (L)	gallon (gal.)
milliliter (mL)	ounce (oz.)

Conversions:

1 bbl. = 31 gal. = 1.173 hL
1 gal. = 128 fl. oz. = 3.785 L
1 oz. = 29.57 mL

Metric and U.S. weight units and abbreviations:

kilogram (kg)	pound (lb.)
gram (g)	ounce (oz.)

Conversions:

1 lb. = 16 oz. = 0.454 kg
1 oz. = 28.35 g

• Most of the concentrations in this book are expressed in weight to volume units. Percentage on the basis of weight to volume is denoted by % (w/v), and is defined by

% (w/v) = g/100 mL = kg/hL.

- Parts per million (ppm) stands for milligrams per liter (mg/L), thus

  $1\% (w/v) = 1$ g/100 mL = 10,000 mg/L = 10,000 ppm.

- Conversion factors for weight to volume concentrations are

  1 g/L = 0.1336 oz./gal.

  and

  1 kg/hL = 2.586 lb./bbl. = 0.0834 lb./gal.

- Volume to volume and weight to weight ratios are also used, primarily for gases. For example, CO_2 levels in the United States are reported in the following units:

  volume of CO_2 = liters of CO_2 per liter of beer.

In Europe, these are expressed in terms of percent by weight:

  % CO_2 (w/w) = grams of CO_2 per 100 grams of beer.

- Since the density of CO_2 is approximately 1.96 grams per liter at room temperature, we have

  volume of CO_2 = (% CO_2 / 100) x (1 / 1.96) x SG x 1,000 = 5.1 x SG x (% CO_2).

- Oxygen is sometimes reported in milliliters per ounce and sometimes in milligrams per liter. These units are related by the following:

  O_2 (mg/L) = O_2 (mL/oz.) x 48.408.

- Many instruments measure the total amount of air in a bottle's headspace and not the O_2 fraction. These are related by the following:

  air (mL/oz.) = O_2 (mg/L) x 0.10338.

This is based on the fact that O_2 is 21% of atmospheric air. It should be noted that the O_2 content of air increases to 32% when dissolved in beer.

*   Water hardness is reported in a variety of units. These and their relationships are

    hardness, mg/L as $CaCO_3$ = (German degree) x 17.9 = (grain/gal.) x 17.1.

Gravity Units

The specific gravity (SG) of a solution is defined as the ratio of the weight of a solution to the weight of an equal volume of water. This is a dimensionless unit being the ratio of two weights. For example, suppose we are measuring in a 500-milliliter flask that weighs 198 grams. Suppose we add 300 milliliters of a solution and find that the flask then weighs 722 grams. This means the weight of the solution is

722 – 198 = 524 g,

and since 500 milliliters of water weighs 500 grams, the SG of the solution is

SG = 524 / 500 = 1.048.

It is worth noting that SG depends on temperature. For example, a solution having a SG of 1.040 at 63 °F (17.5 °C) would have a measured SG of 1.041 had the solution been at 55 °F (13 °C). Alternately, it would have an SG of 1.039 had the solution been at 73 °F (23 °C). In most brewing work, when SGs are quoted without a temperature indication, an ambient temperature of 68 °F (20 °C) is assumed.

The SG of a solution can also be obtained by direct hydrometer measurement. Each instrument has a calibration temperature; to get accurate results, measurements should be done at that temperature. Correction tables are available, but they are not very accurate. It is important to periodically check hydrometer accuracy with direct weight measurements using an accurate balance scale. It is not uncommon for hydrometers to become defective and give false readings.

In evaluating brew house performance, SGs are usually only of indirect interest. What is of interest is the amount of extract present, usually reported as percent on the basis of weight. It is also called degrees extract, or sometimes degrees Brix. Suppose we dissolve 60 grams of sucrose in 440 milliliters of water. Here, extract is the 60 grams of sucrose. Since 440 milliliters (at ambient temperatures) weighs 440 grams, the degrees extract of this solution is

$$[60 / (60 + 440)] \times 100 = 12 \text{ degrees.}$$

The volume of the solution will increase when the sugar is added. Suppose it increases from 440 milliliters to 477 milliliters. Since 477 milliliters of water weighs 477 grams, it follows that the SG of this solution is

$$SG = 500 / 477 = 1.048.$$

Extract in beer or wort is more problematical to define, since both contain a complex spectrum of carbohydrates and other minor solids. Balling greatly simplified the situation by showing that the carbohydrate spectrum could be characterized in terms of an equivalent amount of sucrose. He then repeated the measurements in the above example for various amounts of added sucrose, thereby obtaining a table relating degrees extract to SG. His data had minor errors that were corrected by Plato; therefore, degrees extract (i.e., percent extract) is usually called degrees Balling (°B) or degrees Plato (°P).

Measurements are usually done with a hydrometer or a refractometer. Both actually measure the mixture's SG and use the °B/°P data to convert this to percent extract. This means both are temperature-dependent, although with refractometers, corrections are usually minor since only a drop of solution is used. With hydrometers, temperature effects can be significant and correction data are unreliable. As a consequence, it is best to cool (or heat) the sample to the hydrometer's calibration temperature before making measurements.

It is often useful to express percent extract in a weight to volume basis. The metric conversion to weight/volume (w/v) from weight/weight (w/w) requires only multiplication by the SG:

$$\text{kg extract/hL} = (°P) \times (SG).$$

Table B.1 Extract Data at 68 °F (20 °C)

% Plato	SG	Pounds Extract Per Barrel
0	1.000	0.0
	1.002	1.3
1	1.004	2.6
	1.006	3.9
2	1.008	5.2
	1.010	6.5
3	1.012	7.9
	1.014	9.2
4	1.016	10.5
	1.018	11.9
5	1.020	13.2
	1.022	14.6
6	1.024	15.9
	1.026	17.3
7	1.028	18.6
	1.030	20.0
8	1.032	21.4
	1.034	22.8
9	1.036	24.1
	1.038	25.5
10	1.040	26.9
	1.042	28.3
11	1.044	29.8
	1.046	31.2
12	1.048	32.6
	1.051	34.0
13	1.053	35.4
	1.055	36.9
14	1.057	38.3
	1.059	39.8
15	1.061	41.2
	1.063	42.7
16	1.065	44.2
	1.068	45.6
17	1.070	47.1
	1.072	48.6
18	1.074	50.1
	1.076	51.6
19	1.079	53.1

An Analysis of Brewing Techniques

A wort at 12 °P has a SG of 1.048 (see table B.1), hence a concentration of

12 x 1.048 = 12.58 kg extract/hL

or equivalently, 12.58 grams per 100 milliliters. In the Americas, extract weight to volume is usually expressed in terms of pounds per barrel. Conversions in this case are messy; hence, we included the relevant values along with the °P, and SG data in table B.1.

Mash yields can be computed with the same equation. Take the example in table 1.15 in chapter 1 where we have 1.1 hectoliters of wort at 11.7 °P and a SG of 1.047. This means there is

11.7 x 1.047 = 12.3 kg extract/hL

or

12.3 x 1.1 = 13.5 kg extract

in the sweet wort. Since 20 kilograms of grain were used, the yield is

13.5 x 100 / 20 = 67.5%.

In U.S. units, we have 1.1 barrels of sweet wort with a SG of 11.4 °P (1.046). Referring to table B.1, this is approximately 31 pounds of extract per barrel, a total of

31 x 1.1 = 34 lbs. extract.

Since 50 pounds of malt were used, the yield is (approximately)

34.1 x 100 / 50 = 68%.

Many amateur brewers work entirely with SG, in which case, yield is usually expressed in gravity points (GP). Gravity points are the digits to the right of the decimal point in the SG; thus, wort with a SG of 1.048 has 48 gravity points. Yield in this context is defined as the number of gravity points achieved per grain concentration in pounds per gallon. This number has dimensions of

(GP) / (lbs./gals.) = (GP) x (gals.) / (lbs.),

and it is commonly shortened to "points." To relate this to the notion of yield as previously defined, note that 1 pound per gallon of grain gives Y pounds of extract per gallon, where Y is the standard yield. From table B.1, we see that wort containing 1 pound extract per gallon, which is the same as 31 pounds per barrel, has a SG of 1.046, or 46 gravity points. It follows that

$$(lbs. \times gals.) / lbs. = (Y) \times (0.46)$$

Thus a yield of Y = 65% is equivalent to 65 x 0.46 = 30 points.

pH Basics

At the most intuitive level, pH can be regarded as a measure of acidity. This can be illustrated with a simple example, using three sample solutions:

Solution 1: One liter of pure H_2O
Solution 2: One liter of H_2O and 1 gram of lactic acid (0.055 molar solution)
Solution 3: One liter of H_2O and 0.3 gram of calcium carbonate (0.03 molar solution)

These three solutions can easily be distinguished by taste: solution 1 will be bland and tasteless, solution 2 will have a definite snappy sharpness, while solution 3 will be mouth-coating and chalky. In short, calling the first neutral, the second acidic, and the third alkaline would be consistent with our everyday use of these terms. A detailed chemical analysis would reveal that these solutions differ primarily in their hydrogen ion (H^+) and hydroxide ion (OH^-) contents. In this appendix, these are expressed in moles per liter, denoted by $[H^+]$ and $[OH^-]$, respectively. One mole of a substance has a weight equal to its molecular weight in grams. Hydrogen ions have a molecular weight of (approximately) 1, so 1 mole per liter of hydrogen is the same as 1 gram per liter. The molecular weight of hydroxide ions is 17, so 1 mole per liter of it is the same as 17 grams per liter. In any case, the direct measurements at the standard temperature of 77 °F (25 °C) give the following:

	[H+]	**[OH⁻]**
Solution 1	10^{-7}	10^{-7}
Solution 2	$214 \times 10^{-7} = 10^{-4.67}$	$10^{-9.33}$
Solution 3	$0.005 \times 10^{-7} = 10^{-9.33}$	$10^{-4.67}$

Note that in all cases

$$[H^+] \times [OH^-] = 10^{-14},$$

and because of this, it is convenient to report these concentrations in terms of pH, which is the negative of the exponent of the hydrogen ion concentration. That is

$$pH = -\text{Log } [H^+].$$

This gives pH levels:

Solution 1	7.00
Solution 2	4.67
Solution 3	9.33

More generally, an aqueous solution is considered acidic, neutral, or alkaline if its pH is less than, equal to, or greater than 7.0.

It is also convenient to distinguish strong acids from weak acids. Nitric acid (HNO_3) is an example of the former. When added to water, hydrogen ions will completely dissociate according to the following:

$$HNO_3 \rightarrow H^+ + NO_3^-.$$

Thus, a 0.1 molar solution (which is 3.1 grams per liter) will give a hydrogen ion content of 0.1 mole per liter, hence a pH of 1.0. Lactic acid (LaH, La = $CH_3CHOCOO^-$ = lactate), on the other hand, is an example of a weak acid where the dissociation

$$LaH \leftrightarrow H^+ + La$$

is not complete. In particular, a 0.1 molar solution of it (which is 9 grams per liter) will not give $[H^+] = 0.1$, but something much smaller, namely $[H^+] = 0.009$, which corresponds to

$$pH = 2.04.$$

A simple calculation shows that only 9% of the hydrogen ions dissociated while it was 100% for nitric acid.

All of the acids that are natural to beer are typically weak organic acids. It is the hydrogen ion pool in wort and beer that is crucial to proper enzymatic activity. Since weak acids will not contribute all of their hydrogen ions to the pool, it is important to monitor pH during brewing. Another issue highly relevant to brewing is the presence of strong buffers in beer and wort. Consider a buffer consisting of water, acetic acid, and sodium acetate in the following proportions:

0.05 molar solution of acetic acid (AcH, Ac = CH_3COO^-)
0.01 molar solution of acetate (NaAc).

The pH of this solution should be

pH = 4.75.

Now consider the addition of nitric acid to this solution in small amounts. A 0.001 molar solution of nitric added to water will give a pH of 3.0. However, the addition of the same to the buffer would give

pH = 4.74,

not a significant change. What happens is that the hydrogen ions from HNO_3 are completely dissociating, but then are combining with acetate ions to form acetic acid (AcH). Thus, the titratable amounts of acetic acid will have increased but without any real change in pH. Because mechanisms like this occur throughout brewing, monitoring pH is highly advantageous.

The Mashing Systems section in chapter 1 emphasized that mash pH should be less than 5.5. One of the most important reasons for this is the strong effect the wort hydrogen ion content has on enzyme activity. It has often been stated that since each of the relevant enzymes have different pH optima, any mash pH is necessarily a compromise. However, this does not take into account a crucial property of both amalyase and proteolytic enzymes, namely, their activities do not decrease by much more on the acid side of the optima. But, there is a sharp decrease on the alkaline side. Mathematical models (see Fix 1995) of enzyme kinetics have the following functional form for reaction rates in terms of pH (holding other variables like temperature and mash composition constant).

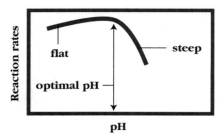

Figure C.1.

In practical terms, this is reflected in a decrease in mash yield with increasing pH:

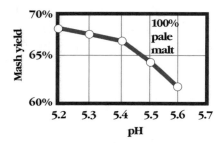

Figure C.2.

Similar results were reported by MacWilliam (1975) and Taylor (1990).

It is well known that the extraction of astringent grain-based constituents is concurrent with an increase in pH of the runoff. Alkaline and/or high temperature sparge water (e.g., greater than 172 °F [78 °C]) will produce this effect. The pH achieved in the mash is also a factor as figure C.3 shows.

Beer fermentation is a natural acidification process, and as a consequence, there is a steady drop in pH during fermentation. Figure C.5 is typical of an ale fermentation at 68 °F (20 °C). Lager fermentations are similar except the times are longer and terminal pH levels are slightly higher.

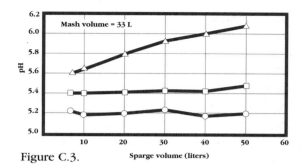

Figure C.3.

The speed of the runoff is also affected by pH. In particular, Taylor (1990) found the following relationship (figure C.4) between grain bed permeability and pH:

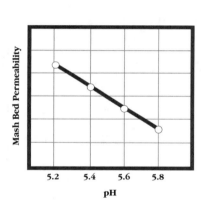

Figure C.4.   Figure C.5.

The biggest drop in pH occurs in the first forty-eight hours. This is desirable, as it strongly inhibits bacterial activity, especially from gram-negative wort spoilers. Of greater importance is that rapid drops in pH correlate with yeast viability and yeast growth, which is why it is important to measure pH on a daily basis. Each yeast strain typically has its own pH attenuation pattern for a given type of wort; therefore, a reduction in the rate of attenuation is usually an early warning sign that a new yeast crop is needed.

The influence of wort composition on pH attenuation in the fermentation is primarily seen in the wort's FAN level. There are two conflicting trends associated with this. Wort amino nitrogen stimulates yeast growth, which in turn promotes pH attenuation. On the other hand, amino acids that are metabolized (such as with very high wort FAN levels) tend to act as pH buffers (among other negative things), and this in turn promotes a resistance to pH attenuation. A balance is needed, which for today's highly modified malt means avoiding excess protein degradation.

Finally, the flavor of the finished beer will also be affected by its pH. As pH falls below 4.0, flavors tend to be sharper and more acidic, with an increased drying aftertaste. Above 4.6, cloying occurs, and mouth-coating effects and chalk/alkaline tones are enhanced. A good deal of variation is found in the pH levels of commercial beers, although there is a lot of similarity within specific beer styles. The data in table C.1 are typical and were taken from Piendl's "Biere aus aller Welt" articles in *Brauindustrie* (1970–1990).

Table C.1 pH Levels of Selected Commercial Beers

Style	pH	Brand
American lager	4.40	Michelob
German Pilsener	4.41	König Pils
Canadian ale	3.80	Molson Export
Bock	4.62	Salvator
English ales	4.20	Whitbread
	3.97	Bass
	4.19	Double Diamond
Alt	4.21	Weihenstephan
Kölsch	4.28	Sion
Weizen	4.32	Spaten Club
Lambic	3.40–3.90	Various
Gueuze	3.32–3.51	Various
Framboise	3.30–3.51	Various

Taylor (1990) reports that both beer haze stability and beer foam stability are affected by pH. Beers with pH levels in the range of 4.5–4.7 had poorer foam and haze stability than equivalent beers with pH values in the range of 4.0–4.4.

The pH of a liquid depends on temperature and will also be influenced by the presence of carbon dioxide. The pH data in this book came from samples that were decarbonated (if necessary) and attemperated to the standard temperature of 77 °F (25 °C) before measurement, in keeping with the standard brewery practice (Harvey 1979).

Appendix D

Prediction and Measurement of RDF

End-point gravities achieved in fermentation can be deceptive indicators of wort's actual fermentability. The point is that final gravities depend on many factors, true wort fermentability is but one. Therefore, other techniques are needed to monitor the RDF associated with different mashing schedules. The simplest and one of the most effective is forced fermentation. Here are the steps involved:

(1) Remove a small amount of wort (typically 1 liter) after cooling.
(2) Pitch a high-attenuation yeast strain (which may or may not be the yeast used in the main fermentation) at ten times the normal rate. Fifty milliliters per liter is a common pitching rate.
(3) Hold the temperature at 77 °F (25 °C) for ale strains, and 68 °F (20 °C) for lager strains.

The conditions created by this procedure usually force the yeast to metabolize all fermentable sugars. Beer aroma at the end of a forced fermentation is extreme, but this is quite normal given the temperatures used.

Alcohol weighs less than water, hence the SG at the forced fermentation end point will not reflect the actual amount of extract present. The °B/°P relationships between SG and percent extract (°P) have been destroyed by the presence of alcohol. As a consequence, the °P associated with end-point SG is called the apparent extract (AE), with

$$ADF = (OE - AE) \times 100 / OE$$

being called the apparent degree of fermentation (ADF) (OE is original extract).

There are two ways to determine the actual amount of residual extract. One way is to remove the alcohol from the sample by (1) carefully recording the volume of the sample, (2) reducing the volume by roughly one-third by boiling it, and (3) carefully replacing the exact volume lost with distilled water.

The °P associated with the SG of the sample after the alcohol is removed is the percent extract based on weight, called the real extract (RE). Real degree of fermentation (RDF) is defined by

$$RDF = (OE - RE) \times 100 / OE$$

To illustrate, the following data were collected from a forced fermentation:

volume = 950 mL
SG = 1.011.

Thus the apparent extract is AE = 2.8 °P. After fifteen minutes of boiling,

volume = 590 mL
percent reduction = 37.9%
SG = 1.017.

Thus the real extract is RE = 4.2 °P.

For beers with alcohol contents less than 5% (by weight), there is a reasonably accurate formula to compute the RE from the OE and the AE, thereby avoiding the boiling procedure:

$$RE = 0.8192 \times AE + 0.1808 \times OE.$$

Measurement of CO_2 and O_2

There are many instruments that measure O_2 and air levels in beer. The most economical, widely accepted, and easy to use in small-scale brewing is the Zahm and Nagel piercing device shown in figure E.1. Place a beer bottle in the stand and lower the crossbar onto the bottle, thereby perforating the crown. The crossbar has lock plates that hold it in position. The needle pierces the closure, and the rubber seal compresses to seal the joint. Temperature and pressure are recorded, and the CO_2 level is determined (table E.1).

The next step is to measure the bottle air level. To do this, open the needle value to allow gas to enter the burette. The latter contains a sodium hydroxide solution that will absorb CO_2 but will allow air to pass through. This causes the liquid to depress, the extent to which is proportional to the volume of air present. The burette on the Zahm and Nagel instrument is calibrated to record air levels in milliliters.

While this instrument is easy to use, the following suggestions will help ensure the best results:

(1) A temperature of 68 °F (20 °C) is a good compromise between two opposing effects: The higher the beer temperature, the easier it is to remove the gas inside the bottle; but the higher the beer

Figure E.1. A Zahm and Nagel air tester.

Table E.1

Temp.												Pounds Pressure		
°F	1	2	3	4	5	6	7	8	9	10	11	12	13	14
30	1.82	1.92	2.03	2.14	2.23	2.36	2.48	2.60	2.70	2.82	2.93	3.02		
31	1.78	1.88	2.00	2.10	2.20	2.31	2.42	2.54	2.65	2.76	2.86	2.96		
32	1.75	1.85	1.95	2.05	2.16	2.27	2.38	2.48	2.59	2.70	2.80	2.90	3.01	
33		1.81	1.91	2.01	2.12	2.23	2.33	2.43	2.53	2.63	2.74	2.84	2.96	
34		1.78	1.86	1.97	2.07	2.18	2.28	2.38	2.48	2.58	2.68	2.79	2.89	3.00
35			1.83	1.93	2.03	2.14	2.24	2.34	2.43	2.52	2.62	2.73	2.83	2.93
36			1.79	1.88	1.99	2.09	2.20	2.29	2.39	2.47	2.57	2.67	2.77	2.86
37				1.84	1.94	2.04	2.15	2.24	2.34	2.42	2.52	2.62	2.72	2.80
38				1.80	1.90	2.00	2.10	2.20	2.29	2.38	2.47	2.57	2.67	2.75
39					1.86	1.96	2.05	2.15	2.25	2.34	2.43	2.52	2.61	2.70
40					1.82	1.92	2.01	2.10	2.20	2.30	2.39	2.47	2.56	2.65
41						1.87	1.97	2.06	2.16	2.25	2.35	2.43	2.52	2.60
42						1.83	1.93	2.02	2.12	2.21	2.30	2.39	2.47	2.56
43						1.80	1.90	1.99	2.08	2.17	2.25	2.34	2.43	2.52
44							1.86	1.95	2.04	2.13	2.21	2.30	2.39	2.47
45							1.82	1.91	2.00	2.08	2.17	2.26	2.34	2.42
46								1.88	1.96	2.40	2.13	2.22	2.30	2.38
47								1.84	1.92	2.00	2.09	2.18	2.25	2.34
48								1.80	1.88	1.96	2.05	2.14	2.21	2.30
49									1.85	1.93	2.01	2.10	2.18	2.25
50									1.82	1.90	1.98	2.06	2.14	2.21
51										1.87	1.95	2.02	2.10	2.18
52										1.84	1.91	1.99	2.06	2.14
53										1.80	1.88	1.96	2.03	2.10
54											1.85	1.93	2.00	2.07
55											1.82	1.89	1.97	2.04
56												1.86	1.93	2.00
57												1.83	1.90	1.97
58												1.80	1.86	1.94
59													1.83	1.90
60													1.80	1.87

©1934, by Zahm & Nagel Co., Inc.

The light table numerals give number of volumes of CO_2 gas at 0 °C-760$_{MM}$ pressure per volume of beer. Chart for use with the Zahm-Hartung CO_2 Volume Meter and Zahm Volume Meter Model "SS-60."

temperature, the greater the pressure and subsequent chance for leakage.

(2) Make sure when the crossbar is lowered that there is a gas-tight seal between the rubber stopper and the bottle cap before engaging the lock plates.

(3) Best results are obtained with a 50–75% NaOH solution in the burette. Gloves, protective clothing, and goggles are essential.

An Analysis of Brewing Techniques

Pounds Pressure															
15	16	17	18	19	20	21	22	23	24	25	26	27	28	29	30
3.02															
2.96															
2.90	3.00														
2.85	2.94														
2.80	2.89	2.98													
2.75	2.84	2.93	3.01												
2.70	2.79	2.87	2.96												
2.65	2.74	2.82	2.91	3.00											
2.60	2.69	2.78	2.86	2.95											
2.56	2.64	2.73	2.81	2.90	2.99										
2.51	2.60	2.68	2.77	2.85	2.94	3.02									
2.47	2.55	2.63	2.72	2.80	2.89	2.98									
2.42	2.50	2.59	2.67	2.75	2.84	2.93	3.02								
2.38	2.46	2.55	2.62	2.70	2.79	2.87	2.96								
2.34	2.42	2.50	2.58	2.66	2.75	2.83	2.91	2.99							
2.30	2.38	2.45	2.54	2.62	2.70	2.78	2.86	2.94	3.02						
2.25	2.34	2.41	2.49	2.57	2.65	2.73	2.81	2.89	2.97						
2.22	2.30	2.37	2.45	2.52	2.61	2.69	2.76	2.84	2.93	3.00					
2.18	2.26	2.33	2.41	2.48	2.57	2.64	2.72	2.80	2.88	2.95					
2.15	2.22	2.29	2.37	2.44	2.52	2.60	2.67	2.75	2.83	2.90	2.98				
2.11	2.19	2.25	2.33	2.40	2.47	2.55	2.63	2.70	2.78	2.85	2.93	3.01			
2.07	2.15	2.21	2.29	2.36	2.43	2.50	2.58	2.65	2.73	2.80	2.88	2.96			
2.04	2.11	2.18	2.25	2.33	2.40	2.47	2.54	2.61	2.69	2.76	2.84	2.91	2.99		
2.00	2.07	2.14	2.21	2.29	2.36	2.43	2.50	2.57	2.64	2.72	2.80	2.86	2.94	3.01	
1.97	2.04	2.11	2.18	2.25	2.32	2.39	2.46	2.53	2.60	2.67	2.75	2.81	2.89	2.96	
1.94	2.01	2.08	2.14	2.21	2.28	2.35	2.42	2.47	2.56	2.63	2.70	2.77	2.84	2.91	2.98

(4) Once the CO_2 is determined, allow the gas to pass into the burette very slowly. If the needle value is opened too quickly, the pressure surge can force some of the CO_2 through the caustic solution, resulting in erroneously high air readings.

References

Allen, F. 1994. *Brewing Techniques* 12:4, 2:5, and 3:6.

———. 1995. *Brewing Techniques* 4:1 and 3:2.

Amerine, M. A., H. W. Berg, and W. V. Cruess. *The Technology of Wine Making*. 1972. Westport, CT.: AVI Publications.

Anderson, S. D., D. Hastings, K. Rossmore, and J. L. Bland. 1995. *MBAA Tech. Quart.* 32:2.

Anger, H. M. 1996. *Brauwelt* 14:2.

Ann Arbor News. 1975. 16 March.

Annemüller, G., and H. J. Manger. 1995. *Brauwelt* 13:2.

ASBC Methods of Analysis. 1958. 6th ed.

ASBC Methods of Analysis. 1992. 8th ed.

Banforth, C. W. 1994. *Brewers Digest* (May).

Beckett, M. H. 1985. *MBAA Tech. Quart.*, vol. 22.

Beer, C. 1989. *MBAA Tech. Quart.*, vol. 26.

Bergen, R. 1993. *Brewing Techniques* 1:3.

Blenkinsop, J. 1991. *MBAA Tech. Quart.*, vol. 28.

Block, S., ed. 1991. *Disinfection, Sterilization, and Presentation*. New York: Lea and Febiger Publications.

Brantley, J. D., and L. Aranha. 1994. *MBAA Tech. Quart.* 31:4.

Brauwelt. 1986. "1985 ED Barley Varieties," vol. 1.

Brauwelt. 1993. "1993 ED Barley Varieties," vol. 5.

Burrel, K., C. Gill, M. McKenchnie, and J. Murray. 1994. *MBAA Tech. Quart.* 31:2.

Casey G. P., and W. M. Ingledew. 1981. *Brewers Digest* (Feb. and April).

———. 1982. *Brewers Digest* (March and April).

Casey, G. P. 1996. *MBAA Tech. Quart.* 33:1.

Chen, E. 1978. *ASBC*, vol. 36.

Christiansen, K. 1995. *MBAA Tech. Quart.* 32:4.

Coors, J. 1977. Chap. 12 in *The Practical Brewer*. Milwaukee: MBAA.

Cowper, J., and R. Taylor. 1988. *MBAA Tech. Quart.* 25:2.

Davis, R. 1987. *Brewers Digest* (May).

Davison, D. 1993. *Homebrew Color Guide.* Greenfield, WI: Davison.

de Clerck, J. 1957. *A Textbook of Brewing,* 2 vols. London: Chapman and Hall.

Derdelinckx, G., B. Vanderhasselt, M. Maudoux, and K. P. Dufour. 1992. *Brauwelt,* vol. 2.

Donhauser S., D. Wagner, and H. Guggels. 1988. Brauwelt Abstracts. *Brauwelt,* vol. 1.

Donhauser, S., and D. Wagner. 1996. *Brauwelt* 14:1.

Feryhough, R., and D. Ryder. 1990. *MBAA Tech. Quart.,* vol. 27.

Fix, G. 1982. *Amateur Brewer,* no. 9.

———. 1985. *Zymurgy* 8:4.

———. 1987. Chap. 12 in *Beer and Brewing.* Boulder: Brewers Publications.

———. 1988. *Beer and Brewing,* vol. 8.

———. 1988. *Zymurgy* 11:3.

———. 1989. *Principles of Brewing Science.* Boulder: Brewers Publications.

———. 1989. *Zymurgy* 12:4.

———. 1991. Chap. 18 in *Beer and Brewing,* vol. 7.

———. 1992. *Zymurgy* 15:3.

———. 1992. *Zymurgy* 15:5.

———. 1993. *Brewing Techniques* 1:1.

———. 1993. *Brewing Techniques* 1:2.

———. 1993. *Crosby and Baker Research Report.*

———. 1993. *UTA Tech. Report,* no. 32.

———. 1993. *Zymurgy* 16:3.

———. 1994. *Brewing Techniques* 2:3.

———. 1995. *The New Brewer* 6:5.

Fix, G., and L. Fix. 1991. *Oktoberfest, Vienna, Märzen,* Boulder: Brewers Publications.

Foster, A., and G. Schmidt. 1994. *Brauwelt,* vol. 2.

Gans, V., S. Gallen, and V. Deak. 1995. *Brauwelt* 13:5.

Garetz, M. 1994. *Using Hops.* Danville, CA: Hop Technical Publications.

Grant, B. 1977. Chap. 8 in *The Practical Brewer.* Milwaukee: MBAA.

Guinard, J. X. 1990. *Lambic.* Boulder: Brewers Publications.

Hagen, B. 1993. *Brauwelt,* vol. 3.

Harvey. J. 1979. Chap. 5 in *Brewing Science.* London: Academic Press.

Haunold, A. 1974. *Crop Sci.,* vol. 14.

Haunold, A., and G. B. Nickerson. 1990. *J. Am. Soc. Brew. Chem.,* vol. 48.

———. 1993. *Brewing Techniques* 1:1.

Heath, H. B. 1988. *Flavor Chemistry and Technology.* Westport, CT: AVI Publishing Co.

Heintz, Q. E. 1987. *MBAA Tech. Quart.,* vol. 24.

Hind, H. L. 1950. *Brewing—Science and Practice.* London: John Wiley.

Huige, N. J. 1992. In *Beer and Wine Production.* ACS Symposium Series.

Hums, J. 1981. *Monatsschrift für,* vol. 34.

Kindraka, J. A. 1987. *MBAA Tech. Quart.,* vol. 24.

———. 1989. *Brewers Digest* (Oct).

Knudsen, F. 1978. *MBAA Tech. Quart.* 15:3.

Kolbach, P. 1953. *Monats. Brau.,* vol. 6.

Larson, J., and H. Brandon. 1988. *MBAA Tech. Quart.* 25:2.

Leeder, G., and M. Girr. 1994. *MBAA Tech. Quart.* 30:2.

Lenahan, R. J. 1992. *MBAA Tech. Quart.* 29:2.

Lodahl, M. 1994. *Brewing Techniques* 2:4 and 2:6.

MacWilliam, J. 1975. *J. Instit. of Brewing,* vol. 81.

Maksuazawa, K., and Y. Nagashima. 1990. *MBAA Tech. Quart.,* vol. 27.

Maksuazawa, K., S. Takahashi, Y. Nagashima, M. Itoh, and K. Yamaudu. 1991. *MBAA Tech. Quart.,* vol. 28.

Meier, P. M., G. P. Jansen, S. Blazka, and R. Hegde. 1995. *MBAA Tech. Quart.* 32:1.

Meilgaard, M. 1991. *MBAA Tech. Quart.,* vol. 28.

Meilgaard, M., C. E. Dalgliesh, and J. F. Clapperton. 1979. *J. ASBC* 37:1.

Mellon, J. 1995. *Zymurgy* (Fall).

Melm, G., P. Tung, and A. Pringle. *MBAA Tech. Quart.* 32:1.

Miller, D. 1993. *Brewing Techniques* 1:3.

Mitter, M. 1995. *Brauwelt,* vol. 4.

Moll, M. 1979. Chap. 7 in *Brewing Science.* London: Academic Press.

Morton, B. J., and M. R. Sfat. 1986. *MBAA Tech. Quart.* 23:1.

Nagami, J. 1980. *MBAA Tech. Quart.* 17:2.

Narziss, L. 1992. *Brauwelt,* vol. 4.

———. 1993. *Brauwelt,* vol. 3.

———. 1993. *Brauwelt,* vol. 5.

———. 1993. *Zymurgy* (Winter).

Narziss, L., H. Miedaner, and F. Schneider. 1992. *Brauwelt,* vol. 4.

Nathan, L. 1927. Patent of the United Kingdom.

———. 1930. *J. Instit. of Brewing,* vol. 36.

Neve, R. A. 1991. *Hops.* London: Chapman and Hall.

Nugy, A. L. 1948. *Brewers Manual.* Bayonne, NJ: Jersey Publications.

Oliver and Dauman, B. 1988. *Brauwelt,* vol. 3.

———. 1988. *Brauwelt,* vol. 4.

Oloff, K., and A. Piendl. 1978. *Brewers Digest* (March).

One Hundred Years of Brewing. 1974. New York: Arno Press.

Owades, J., and M. Plam. 1988. *MBAA Tech. Quart.* 25:4.

O'Connor-Cox, E., J. Lodolo, G. Steyn, and B. Axcell. 1996. *MBAA Tech. Quart.* 33:1.

Peacock, V. E. 1992. *MBAA Tech. Quart.* 29:3.

Peacock, V. E., and M. L. Deinzer. 1981. *J. Am. Soc. Br. Chem.*, vol. 39.

Piendl, A. 1970–1990. "Biere aus Aller Welt" columns in *Brauindustrie*.

Piesley, J. 1977. Chap. 11 in *The Practical Brewer*. Milwaukee: MBAA.

Poirier, M. X., and F. Lang. 1978. *MBAA Tech. Quart.* 15:3.

Preis, F., and W. Mitter. 1995. *Brauwelt*, vol. 4.

Protz, R. 1991. *European Beer Almanac*. Mottaf, Scotland: Lochar Publications.

———. 1991. *Real Ale*. Mottaf, Scotland: Lochar Publications.

Raible, K. 1984. *Brauwelt*, vol. 2.

Raines, M. B. 1992. *Yeast Culturing*. Camarillo, CA: Brewers Resource.

———. 1992. *Zymurgy* (Special Issue).

———. 1995. *Laboratory Manual*. Boulder: Brewers Publications.

———. 1996. Conversation with author.

Reuther, H., and H. Brandon. 1994. *MBAA Tech. Quart.* 31:1.

Richman, D. 1994. *Bock*. Boulder: Brewers Publications.

Rigby, L. 1972. *ASBC Proc.*, vol. 30.

Robinson, J. 1982. *Connoisseur's Guide to Beer*. Aurora, IL: CH Publications.

Ruggiero, D., J. Spillane, and D. Snyder. 1995. *Zymurgy* (Fall).

Russel, I. 1995. Chap. 10 in *Handbook of Brewing*. New York: Maval Dekker.

Ryder, D., C. R. Davis, D. Anderson, F. M. Glancy, and J. N. Power. 1988. *MBAA Tech. Quart.*, vol. 25.

Scheer, F. 1990. *MBAA Tech. Quart.* 27:73–75.

———. 1990. *The New Brewer*. 7:4.

Schmidt, H. J. 1995. *Brauwelt*, vol. 2.

———. 1995. *Brauwelt* 13:2.

Schröder, W. 1984. *Brauwelt*, vol. 1.

Siebel Institute of Technology. Short Course on Brewing Microbiology.

Siebert, K. J., and E. J. Knudsen. 1989. *MBAA Tech. Quart.*, vol. 26.

Sorensen, I., L. de Verno, and S. Lord. 1983. *Brewers Digest* (September).

Taylor, D. G. 1990. *MBAA Tech. Quart.*, vol. 27.

Taylor, D. G., P. Bamber, J. W. Brown, and J. P. Murray. 1982. *MBAA Tech. Quart.* 29:4.

Uhlig, G. 1992. *Brauwelt*, vol. 4.

Unterstein, K. 1994. *Brauwelt* 12:4.

Verzeli, M., and D. de Keukeleire. 1991. *Chemistry and Analysis of Hop and Beer Bitter Acids*. Amsterdam: Elsevier.

Vogel, E. H., F. H. Schwaiger, H. G. Leonhardt, and J. A. Merten. 1946. *The Practical Brewer*. Milwaukee: MBAA.

Wackerbauer, K. 1986. *Brauwelt*, vol. 1.

———. 1992. *Brauwelt*, vol. 1.

———. 1993. *Brauwelt*, vol. 3.

References

Wackerbauer, K., and U. Balzer. 1992. *Brauwelt,* vol. 2.

Wainwright, T. 1973. *J. Instit. of Brewing,* vol. 79.

Warner, E. 1992. *German Wheat Beer.* Boulder: Brewers Publications.

Wiegmann, D. 1912–1913. *All gemcine Brauer—U. Hopfenzeitung.*

Woodward, J. D. 1978. *Brewers Digest* (May).

Zattler, F., and G. Krauss. 1970. *Monat. Brau,* vol. 23.

Zimmermann, A. 1904. Brauereibi Briebslehre. Buffalo, NY: Self published.

Zymurgy. 1990. (Special Hop Issue).

Index

A

Acetaldehyde, 102, 142
Acids
  acetolactic, 101
  alpha/beta/gamma, 34, 35, 36, 37
  amino, 23
  citric, 123
  food-grade, 20
  gibberellic, 3
  iso-alpha, 34, 35, 49
  lactic, 20, 117, 166
  measuring, 165
  nitric, 112, 166, 167
  organic, 123
  peracetic, 114–15, 116
  phosphoric, 112, 113, 123
  silicic, 127
  tartaric, 123
Acridine orange, 87
Acti-Dione, 95, 145, 146
Ad-humulone, 35
Ad-lupulone, 36
Aeration
  hot-side, 25
  wort, 81, 99–100
  yeast, 79–80
Agar, 82, 145, 146, 147 (table)
Alcohols
  aliphatic, 96

  D-values for, 116
  fusel, 56, 95, 96–98, 97 (table), 142
  isopropyl, 116
  phenol, 95, 96, 97–98
Aldehydes, 125
Alexis barley, 1
Alkalinity, 16, 17, 168
  criterion for, 18–19
  residual, 18, 19, 20
Alpha-amylase activity, optimal
    range for, 25
Ambient oxygenation systems,
    problems with, 79
American Society of Brewing
    Chemists (ASBC) Methods
    of Analysis, 142
Anchor Brewery, 104
Antifoaming agents, 113, 115
Apparent attenuation, 56
Apparent degree of fermentation
    (ADF), 172
Aroma, 171
Aroma hops, 33, 37, 43–44, 46
Assortment, 4
Aura malt, 1
Austin wheat yeast strain, 64–65
Australian/Cooper yeast strain, 64
Autocarbonation, described, 133

B

Back-flushing, 128
Bacteria, 89
   in bottling, 137
   haze and, 119
   thermophilic, 118
Bacto Universal Beer Agar
   Medium, 82
Ballantine/Chico yeast strain, 60
Barley
   protein levels, 1–2, 2 (table)
   unmalted, 11, 12, 13
Barley wines, 79
B-brite, rating for, 111 (table)
Beechwood chips, fining with, 126
Beer profiles, conceptualizing, 149
Beer's law, 143
Beer stone, 112
Belgian ales, fruitiness in, 136
Belgian ale yeast strain, 65
Belgian lambic yeast strain, 65
Belgian-style white beer, 13
Beta-amylase activity, optimal
   range for, 25
Beta-glucan, 24
   degradation of, 5, 13
   extraction of, 119
Beta-glucanase, 24, 27
Bicarbonate, effect of, 21
"Biere aus aller Welt" (Piendl),
   102, 170
Bittering units (BU), 34–35, 49, 141
   calculation of, 48
Blowtorches, 71, 73 (photo), 83
Bock (Richman), 31
Body, filtration and, 129
Bottle refermentation, 135–37
   carbon-dioxide levels in, 136–37
   characteristics of, 136
Bottling, 134, 137–40
   air ingress during, 137
Brambling Cross hops, 44
Brettanomyces, 94, 95

Brett signature, 94
Brewer's Gold, development of, 43
Brewer's jar, 145, 145 (photo)
Brewers Resource, 57
BrewTech, 57, 58, 59, 61, 62, 63, 64, 65
Brushes, 132
Burton ale yeast strain, 62
Burton sulfur taste, 21
Burton water, 21 (table)

C

Calcium chloride, 19, 20
Calcium sulfate, 20
California Steam yeast strain, 59
Caloric value, measuring, 141–42
Canadian ale yeast strain, 61
Candida, 95
Carbohydrate yield, 22
Carbonation, 77, 130–37
   artificial/natural, 135
Carbon dioxide, 96, 130–31
   direct injection of, 132–34, 135
   levels of, 130 (table)
   measurement of, 173–75
   residual, 137
   transferring beer via, 133
Cartridges, 128 (photo)
   ceramic/stainless, 128
Caryophylene, 38
Cascade hops, 40
Category 1000, 147, 147 (fig.)
Category 2000, 147, 148 (fig.)
Category 3000, 148 (fig.)
Category 4000, 148 (fig.)
Category 5000, 148 (fig.), 152
Category 6000, 148 (fig.), 152
Category 7000, 148 (fig.)
Category 8000, 149 (fig.), 151
Caustics, 111
   rating for, 111 (table)
Cell counts
   concentration of, 86, 86 (fig.)

microscopic, 84
volumetric determination of, 69
Cell growth, propagation and, 70
Cell viability, staining and, 87
Cereal grains, 10-14
Chilled wort, oxygenation of, 75-81
Chill proofing, 13, 119
Chlorine, sanitizing with, 116
Christian Schmidt yeast strain, 55, 59
    substrains of, 56 (table)
Chromatography, 45, 49
Classic aroma hops, 39 (table)
    quality factors of, 39
Cleaning agents
    quick and easy, 118
    types of, 109-12
Climatization, propagation and, 70
Cluster hops, 42, 43
Co-humulone, 35-36, 41, 46
Color, 7 (table)
    malt, 4
    measuring, 142, 143-44
Columbus hops, 41
Co-lupulone, 36
Competitions, 154
    improving, 153, 155-56
Compressed air, yeast and, 78
Contaminates, 120
    categories of, 14
    cleaning, 109, 110
Continental Pilseners,
    evaluation of, 155 (fig.)
Coors Brewing Company,
    filtering at, 128
Copper, wort and, 15
Corn grits, refined, 11, 12
Corn starch, refined, 12
Counterpressure, 138
Counterpressure fill, 138
Counterpressure filler, 138 (photo)
Cross-flow filters, 126, 126 (fig.), 128
Crystal hops, 41
Cytolysis, 4-5, 8

D

Dark ales, water for, 20
Davison color chart, 144
Deadhead filters, 126, 126 (fig.), 127
De Clerck, J., 2, 8, 104, 115
    theory of, 45, 46
Deionization, 15-16
Dekkera, 94
Detergents, 109
    aspects of, 110-11
    ratings for, 111 (table)
Diacetyl, 10, 55, 56, 58, 62, 100-102
    in pitching yeast, 101
    precursors of, 101
Diastic power, 7 (table)
Diffusing stone, 76
Dimethyl sulfide (DMS), 21, 52, 53, 104
    creation of, 51
    monitoring, 8
    reduction, 45, 49-51
Dissolved oxygen, 80
    yeast and, 78
DLG system, 149
DMS. *See* Dimethyl sulfide
Donhauser, S., 80
Dry heat, sterilization with, 117
Dry hopping, 45, 46, 49
    first-wort hopping and, 47
Drying, 4
Duvel yeast strain, 65
D-values, 113, 114, 115, 116, 117, 118

E

East Kent Goldings, 44
    flavor from, 150
Emulsification, 110, 111
End-point gravities, 171
English-style extra special bitter
    flavors in, 149, 150, 151
    gravity of, 152
    intensity levels of, 150 (fig.)
Enzymes, fining with, 125

Escherichia coli, 92, 103, 113
Essential oils, 37–39
Ester, 38, 56, 58, 60, 62, 75, 98–99
  formation of, 99–100
  levels of, 98 (table), 99 (table)
  wort oxygen levels and, 100 (table)
Etched grid, magnification of, 85 (fig.)
Ethanol, 102, 140
Ethyl caproate, 136
Evaluation, 141–55
  bias in, 153 (table), 154 (table)
  weighted system for, 155–56
Evaporation rate, 54
Extract, 6
  data for, 162 (table)

F

FAN. *See* Free amino nitrogen level
Farnasene, 38, 40, 41, 152
Feed and bleed system, 133–34,
  134 (photo)
Feed and rock system, 133
Fermentation, 74, 119, 168
  aeration during, 80
  aerobic/anaerobic, 80
  by-products of, 96–104
  dysfunctional, 122
  forced, 141, 172
  open/closed, 107
  primary, 126
  secondary, 135
  temperature for, 99, 99 (table)
  zinc and, 15
Fermentation vessels, 104–8
  stirring devices for, 106
Ferments, trial, 106 (table)
Filters
  micron rating of, 128
  types of, 126 (fig.), 126–27, 128
Filtration, 5, 15–16, 120, 126–30
  activated carbon, 15
  effects of, 128–30, 129 (table)

problems with, 129
  submicron, 130
Fine/coarse grind extract,
  differences in, 7 (table)
Fining agents, 119–26
First Gold hops, 44
First-wort hopping, 46–47
  dry hopping and, 47
Fisher Scientific, 77
Flaked maize, 11
Flaked rye, 13–14
Flasks, 71, 72 (photo)
  inoculation of, 73
Flavor, 33
  BU and, 35
  blindness to, 153
  evaluation of, 142, 146–54
  filtration and, 129
  stability, 138–39
Flavor wheel, 147, 147 (fig.)
Flocculation, 56, 93
Foam
  harming, 131–32, 132 (table)
  inducing, 138
  iodophors and, 114
  stability, 170
Food Research Institute, 57, 63
Formazin Turbidity Units, 120, 121, 124
  visual description of, 121 (table)
Four-vinyl guaiacol levels, 98
Free amino nitrogen (FAN) level,
  6, 6 (table), 23, 122, 170
Friability, 5
Fuggles hops, 40, 44
Fusel alcohols, 56, 95, 96–98, 142
  levels of, 97 (table)
  yeast and, 97
Fusel oils, 96

G

Gelatin, fining with, 123–24
Gelatinization, 10–11, 12

Geraniol, 38, 40
German Alt yeast strain, 61
German Kölsch yeast strain, 60–61
German lagers, carbon dioxide in,
    131 (table)
German purity law, 124, 127
German wheat beer
    bottle refermentation for, 136
    carbon dioxide in, 131 (table)
Germination, time/cost of, 3
Glassware, 71, 72 (photo)
    dirty, 132
Glucanase enzymes, 25
Glycogen, iodine test for, 87–89
Goldings, 21, 44
    flavor from, 150
Grain assortment data, 5 (table)
Grain bed permeability, pH and,
    169, 169 (fig.)
Gram-negative bacteria, 103, 113,
    115, 116
    test for, 92–93
Gram-positive bacteria, 113, 115, 116
    testing for, 89–92
Gravity units, 160–64
Green Bullett hops, 43
Guinness yeast strain, 63

H

Hallertau hops, 40, 41, 43
Hallertau Huller hops, 43
Hallertau Magnum hops, 43
Hallertau Traditional hops, 43
Halogen sanitizers, 114, 116
    iodine-based, 113
Hansenula, 95
Hard water
    permanently, 17
    temporary, 16–17
Hartong index, 7
Haze, 121
    biological, 119

chill, 13, 120
    nonculture yeast and, 119
    oxidation, 120
    stability, 170
Hemocytometer, 84, 84 (photo),
    85, 87
    diagram of, 84 (fig.)
Herald hops, 44
Heterocyclic compounds,
    sulfur-bearing, 52, 53 (table)
High-alpha level hops, U.S.,
    42 (table)
Hind, H. Lloyd, viii
HLP media. *See* Hsu's *Lactobacillus
    Pediococcus* media
Hop additions, controlling, 45–47
Hop bitterness, intensity of, 35
Hop extraction, 45, 47–49
Hop oil, 45–46, 49
Hopping
    dry, 45, 46, 47, 49
    first-wort, 46–47
    late, 45–46
    post-fermentation, 46, 49
Hops, 33–44
    varieties of, 39–44
    special, 40 (table)
Hormones, 3
Hsu's *Lactobacillus Pediococcus*
    (HLP) media, 89, 90,
    90 (photo), 91, 92, 144
    chemical makeup of, 89 (table)
Hsu's *Lactobacillus Pediococcus*
    (HLP) tubes, 90, 90 (photo)
Hums, J., 124
Humuladienone, 39
Humulene, 38, 39
Humulene epoxides, 39
Humulenol, 39
Humulone, 35
Hydrocarbons, 38
Hydrogels, 125
Hydrogen ions, 165, 166, 167

Hydrogen sulfide
  curve, 103 (fig.)
  yeast growth and, 103
Hydrometers, 160, 161
Hydroxide ions, 165

I

ID jar. *See* Internal diameter jar
India pale ale, flavor for, 149
Infection, defending against, 109
Inocluation, slant, 81–84
Inoculation loops, 71, 72, 73 (photo), 83
Inorganic material
  cleaning, 109, 110
  contamination by, 14, 120
Internal diameter (ID) jar, 142
Iodine, 113
  D-values of, 114
Iodophors, 115
  beer foam and, 114
  D-values for, 114 (table)
  versions of, 113–14
Irish moss, fining with, 121–22,
    122 (table)
Isinglass, 124, 126
  fining with, 122–23, 123 (table)
  ready-to-use, 123
Iso-ad-humulone, 35
Iso-alpha concentration, 48
Isoamyl acetate, 136
Iso-co-humulone, 35
Isoelectric points, 121
Iso-humulone, 35

J

Judging, improving, 153, 155–56

K

Kettle utilization rate (KUR), 47
  estimation of, 48, 48 (table)

Kieselguhr filtration, 124, 125
  first/second pre-coats in, 127 (fig.)
  problems with, 128
  protocol for, 127
Kilning, 4
  temperatures for, 7–8
Knudsen, F.
  tank hydraulics and, 106
Kolbach index, 5–6, 5 (table), 18,
    27, 33
König Pils, 21
Kraeusening, 134–35
KUR. *See* Kettle utilization rate

L

Lactobacillus, 89, 92, 145
Lactobacillus delbrueckii, 92
Lactobacillus pastorianus, 146
Lagers
  continental-style, 152
  water for, 20
Lang, F., 55
Lautering, 5, 30
Liberty Ale, 61
Liberty hops, 41
Light amber ales, water for, 20
Linalool, 38, 40
Liquid yeast, storing, 67
London ale yeast strain, 62
Lovibond 52 scale, 142, 143,
    143 (table)
Lublin hops, 43–44
Lupulone, 36

M

Maillard reactions, 45, 52–54
Malt, 1–10
  barley, 1, 8
  brown, 10
  caramel, 10
  crystal, 10

green, 9, 9 (table)
pale, 4
Pilsener, 4, 27
protein in, 2
regular, 9, 10 (table)
roasted, 4, 9–10
storage of, 10, 11
sulfur content of, 7–8
Vienna, 4
wheat, 8–9
Malt/agar solution, 82
Malt extract, 82
Malting, 2–4
floor, 3, 3 (photo)
modification indices for, 4–8
pneumatic, 3
Maltose, 23, 25
Maltose/maltotriose ratios, 23, 25
Maltotriose, 23, 25, 93, 137
Malt sulfur levels, 8 (table)
Mash
EBC, 5
infusion, 31
single-temperature, 30
three-temperature, 30
Mashing systems, 6, 9, 11, 25,
22–28, 30–31, 33, 26, 167
choosing, 22–23
Mash pH, 18, 19, 33, 141
controlling, 24
Mash yield
computing, 163
pH and, 168, 168 (fig.)
Maximum dissolved oxygen,
wort/temperature/SGs and,
76 (fig.)
Measurements
basic units of, 157–59
conversions for, 157, 158
Media, preparation of, 82–84
Megasphaeria, 103, 145
Meilgaard, Morton, 147
Meilgaard's system, 146–54

physiological factors of, 153 (table)
psychological factors of, 154 (table)
Melanoidins, 4, 52
removing, 125
Metals
haze-forming, 120
maximum acceptable levels of,
14 (table)
Methylene blue, 87
Metric units, prefixes for, 157
Microbes, 113, 139–40
contamination by, 14
flavoring and, 15
Microbiological analysis, 140,
144–45
Micropipettes, 84, 85
Microscopes, 84, 88 (photo)
Mineral content, 17 (table)
Moderate alpha bittering hops,
42 (table)
Moist heat, sterilization with, 117
Mold contamination, 139–40
Moll, M., 22
Monoterpenes, 38
Mount Hood hops, 41
Mutants, testing for, 93–94
Mutated culture yeast, haze and, 119
MYGP medium, 93, 94
Myrcene, 38

N

Nachweismedium für
Bierschadliche Bacterium, 144
Narziss, L., 10
on mashing, 11
Nathan, L.
unitank and, 104
N-heterocyclics, 31
Nicotinamido adenine dinucleotide
(NADH), 87
95-131-140-158 program, 31,
32 (fig.)

Noble-type hops, 40, 41, 152
    U.S. versions of, 41 (table)
Nonhumulone bitter substances,
    36, 37
Northern Brewer hops, 40
North German lager yeast, 58
Norwich NCYC 1187 yeast strain, 63
Nylon 66, 124

O

Obesumbacterium, 92
Off-flavors, indicator substances for,
    52–54
Oils, 33
    essential, 37–39
    fusel, 96
    hop, 45–46, 49
Olympic hops, 41
Omega hops, 44
104–122–140–158 program, 26 (fig.)
140–122–158 program, 29 (fig.)
150 (66) program, 32 (fig.)
Organic material
    cleaning, 109
    contamination by, 14
    flavoring and, 15
Organoleptic analysis, 46
Overfiltration, problems with, 126
Overpitching, 68, 81
Oxidized polyphenols, removing, 125
Oxygen, 38
    measurement of, 78, 173–75
    yeast, 79–80
Oxygen demand, 75
    yeast, 76, 79

P

Pale ales, water for, 20
Pasteur effect, 80
PBW, 111
    rating for, 111 (table)

Pectinatus, 51, 103, 145
Pediococcus, 89, 92, 145
Pediococcus damnosus, 116
Percent alcohol by weight, 158
    measuring, 141–42
Percent extract, SG and, 171, 172
Perle hops, 40
Perlite, 127
Permanent palate bias, 152
pH, 141, 170 (table)
    basics of, 165–70
    controlling, 145
    drop in, 169, 170
    grain bed permeability and, 169,
        169 (fig.)
    mash yield and, 168, 168 (fig.)
    reaction rates and, 168, 168 (fig.)
    for selected commercial beers,
        170 (table)
    water, 114
    wort composition and, 169
    yeast growth and, 169
    yeast viability and, 169
Phoenix hops, 44
Physiological factors, 152–54,
    153 (table)
Piendl, A., 102, 170
Pilsener
    flavor profile of, 151 (fig.), 152
    water for, 21
Pilsner Urquell, water for, 21
Pioneer hops, 44
Pipettes, 90, 91
Pitching, 68–69, 74, 80–81, 83,
    89, 137
Pitching yeast, 92
    diacetyl in, 101
    evaluating, 84–95
Plate and frame filters, 127–28
Poirier, M. X., 55
Polyclar AT, fining with, 124–25
Polyphenols, 119, 120
Polyvinylpyrrolidone, 124

An Analysis of Brewing Techniques

Pouring, improper, 132
Povidone, 124, 125
Pre-evacuation, 137, 138
Pregelatinized flakes, 12–13
Presentation order, effects of,
    154 (table)
Pride of Ringwood hops, 43
Profiles, conceptualizing, 149
Progress hops, 44
Propagation, stages of, 70–75, 83
Protein content, 10, 23
Protein degradation, 5, 25, 131
Protein modification, 6, 7, 9, 27,
    28, 30
Proteolysis, 5
Psychological factors, 152–54,
    154 (table)

Q

Quality, viii, 2
    data for, 141
    indices of, vii
Quaternary ammonium compounds
    (Quats), 115, 116
    D-values for, 115 (table)
    mopping with, 140

R

Raines, M. B., 80
Rainier Brewery, 104
Rauchbier, 10
Raw grits, 11
Reaction rates, pH and, 168, 168 (fig.)
Real degree of fermentation (RDF),
    22, 23, 25, 26, 28, 94
    controlling, 24
    measurement of, 171–72
    prediction of, 171–72
Real extract (RE), computing, 172
Refermentation, bottle, 135–37
Refractometers, 161

Repitching, 67–68, 101
Resins, 33, 34–37
Respiratory deficiencies, 93, 94
Reverse osmosis, 15
Rhodamine B, preparation of, 87
Rice grits, 11
Richman, Darryl, 31
Rigby, L., 36
Ringwood yeast strain, 63–64
Rinsability, 110, 111
Russian Serebrianka hops, 40
Rye adjuncts, 11, 13–14

S

Saaz hops, 40, 43, 44, 152
Saccharification, 10–11, 12
Saccharomyces cerevesia, 60
Saccharomyces diastaticus, 94
Saccharomyces ludwigie, 98
Sanitizers, 68, 112–18
    thermal, 117 (table)
Saponification, 110
Saxe, Marshal, viii
Schlitz Brewing Company, 106
Scottish ale yeast strain, 61–62
Selectivity, propagation and, 70
Sequestering agents, 112, 112 (table)
Sesquiterpenes, 38, 41
SG. See Specific gravity
Shock excretion, 66
Sicklebract hops, 43
Siebel Institute of Technology,
    57, 59, 62, 65, 144
Silica gel, fining with, 125
Slants, preparation of, 81–84
S-methyl methionine (SMM), 50
S-methyl methionine (SMM)
    to dimethyl sulfide (DMS)
    conversion curve, 51 (fig.)
Sodium hypochlorite, 116
Sodium ions, role of, 21–22
Solman, 43

Soluble to total protein ratio (S/T), 5
Spalt Select hops, 43
Sparging, 26, 168
Specific gravity (SG), 76, 130, 142,
    160, 161, 163-64
    percent extract and, 171, 172
Spectrophotometry, 143-44
Spulboy system, 132
Squat fermenter, 105, 106,
    106 (photo)
Stability, 56-57
Staining
    cell viability via, 87
    dyes for, 87, 88 (photo)
Staling, 120, 136, 138, 139, 149
    formation of, 139 (fig.)
Starch modification, 6, 7
Sterilization, 112, 114, 144
Stirring devices, 106
Storage
    malt, 11
    yeast, 65-68, 66 (table)
Straub Brewing Company, 21
Stroh's Brewing Company, 106
Styrian Goldings, 44
Sulfur, 21, 150
Sulfur compounds, 56, 58, 102-4,
    104 (table), 142, 152
    reduction of, 103
Superattenuators, 94
Surfactance, 110, 111
Syringes, 90, 91

T

Tall fermenters, 106, 107
Tank hydraulics, 105-6, 107 (fig.)
Target hops, 44
Temperature
    controlling, 24, 26
    fermentation, 56, 99, 99 (table)
    programs, 4 (table), 24-28,
        30-31, 33

Temporary palate bias, 152
Test batch 150 (66) results, 30 (table)
Test batch series 1, 27, 28 (table)
Test batch series 2, 27-28, 29 (table)
Test batch series 3, 30-31,
    31 (table), 33
Test brew, 49 (table)
Test tubes, 82, 90, 91
    heating, 90 (photo)
    with 1-milliliter sample, 91 (photo)
    water bath for, 91 (photo)
Tettnanger hops, 41, 44, 152
Thermal sanitation,
    D-values/Z-values for, 117 (table)
Thermal stress, sensitivity to, 139
Time
    controlling, 24
    programs, 4 (table)
Transfer box, 70-71, 71 (photo),
    72, 83
Triangle tests, 100, 155
Trichloroanisole, 140
Trisodium phosphate (TSP), 111
    rating for, 111 (table)
Triumph malt, 1
Trub carry-over, 79
Tryptophol, 95
Turbidity, 119
Tyrosol, 95

U

UK ales, carbon dioxide in,
    131 (table)
Ultra hops, 41
Underpitching, 68, 74, 75, 87
Unitank, 77 (photo), 104, 107, 119
    height to diameter ratio for, 105,
        105 (fig.)
    recirculating, 108 (fig.)
Universal brewer's agar, 145, 146
    composition of, 147 (table)
Unterstein, K., 105

V

Valine, 102
Variables, measurement of, viii
Vegetation process, 3
Veltins, water for, 21
Verogels, 125
Vinegar, 111
Vino strains, 94, 95
Volumetric determination,
     accuracy of, 69
Volumetric units, 157
Volume units, defining, 157–58

W

Wackerbauer, K., 37
Wagner, D., 80
Warner, E., 137
Washing sodas, 111
     rating for, 111 (table)
Water, 14–22
     acidification, 19–20
     classic brewing center, 19 (table)
     maximum acceptable metal
          levels in, 14 (table)
     mineral content of, 17 (table),
          17–18
Water baths, 91 (photo)
     guidelines for, 93 (table)
Water lines, sanitary, 16
Weight units, 157
Weihenstephan W-68 yeast strain,
     57, 59, 61, 64
Wetting power, 110
Wheat adjuncts, 11, 13
Wheat beer
     bottle refermentation for, 136
     carbon dioxide in, 130 (table)
     yeast for, 58
Whitbread yeast strain, 63
White beer, Belgian-style, 13
White Labs, 57, 58, 59, 61, 62, 63,
     64, 65

Wort
     copper content of, 15
     protein-deficient, 122
Wort aeration, 81
     ester formation and, 99–100
Wort boiling, 31, 35, 44–54
     Maillard reactions and, 52–54
Worthington's White Shield, 62
Wort oxygenation, 76, 81, 81 (table)
     ester and, 100 (table)
     strong/weak, 77
Wort pH, 18, 24, 169
     controlling, 37
     fermented, 141
Wyeast Laboratories, 57, 58, 59,
     61, 62, 63, 64, 65, 82

Y

Yeast, viii, 6, 23, 55–65, 88 (photo),
     117–19
     aeration of, 79–80
     ale, 60–65
     classification of, 55
     collecting, 67–68
     diacetyl in, 101
     dissolved oxygen and, 78
     ester levels of, 99 (table)
     evaluating, 84–95
     first-generation, 74
     functional attributes of, 56–57
     fusel alcohol and, 97
     haze and, 119
     high-gravity beers and, 79
     hydrogen sulfide and, 103
     inoculation of, 70, 91
     lager, 57–58
     limits on, 68
     liquid, 67
     oxygenation of, 79–80
     physiological condition of, 75
     pitching/repitching, 67–68,
          84–95, 101

propagation of, 70–75
sources of, 57
stability of, 68
starters, 81
storing, 65–68, 66 (table)
tests for, 94–95
Yeast growth
 pH and, 169
 stimulating, 81
Yeast Labs, 57, 58, 59, 61, 62, 63, 64, 65
Yeast propagator, 75, 75 (photo)
Yeast slurry, 69 (photo)
Yeast viability, pH and, 169
Yeoman hops, 44

Z

Zahm and Nagel, 129
 air tester, 173 (photo)
 cartridge filter, 128
 feed and bleed system, 134, 134 (photo)
 piercing device, 173
 tank, 76, 77, 77 (photo), 78, 106 (photo)
Zinc
 concentration of, 14–15
 fermentation and, 15
Z-value, 117, 118
Zymomonas, 102

An Analysis of Brewing Techniques